True Stories
5

Sandra Heyer

True Stories: Level 5, Silver Edition

Pearson Education, 221 River Street, Hoboken, NJ 07030

Staff Credits: The people who made up the ***True Stories: Level 5, Silver Edition*** team, representing content creation, design, manufacturing, marketing, multimedia, project management, publishing, rights management, and testing, are Pietro Alongi, Tracey Cataldo, Dave Dickey, Warren Fischbach, Lucy Hart, Gosia Jaros-White, Barry Katzen, Linda Moser, Dana Pinter, Paula Van Ells, Joseph Vella, and Peter West.

Text design and layout: Don Williams
Composition: Page Designs International
Project supervision: Bernard Seal
Contributing editors: Françoise Leffler and Bernard Seal

Cover images: *(from top to bottom)* budabar/123RF; deepstock/Shutterstock; Herschel Hoffmeyer/Shutterstock; KK Tan/Shutterstock; Monkey Business Images/Shutterstock; *(silver edition badge)* deepstock/Shutterstock

Library of Congress Cataloging-in-Publication Data

A catalog record for the print edition is available from the Library of Congress.

Printed in the United States of America

ISBN-13: 9780137598892 (Student Book and eBook with Digital Resources and Pop-Up Stories)
ISBN-10: 0137598890 (Student Book and eBook with Digital Resources and Pop-Up Stories)

ISBN-13: 9780137599158 (eBook with Digital Resources and Pop-Up Stories)
ISBN-10: 0137599153 (eBook with Digital Resources and Pop-Up Stories)

21 2025

CREDITS

PHOTO CREDITS

Page ix: Courtesy of Sandra Heyer; **2:** Dudabar/123RF; **4:** Claudio zaccherini/Shutterstock; **9:** Alexey Butenkov/123RF; **13:** *(tl)* Antonio Diaz/123RF, *(tr)* Dolgachov/123RF, *(bl)* Pressmaster/Shutterstock, *(br)* Miodrag ignjatovic/E+/Getty Images; **18:** © Joe Musso, 2018; **20:** Miguel Soutullo/Shutterstock; **25:** KK Tan/Shutterstock; **29:** Zerocreatives/Westend61 GmbH/Alamy Stock Photo; **34:** Paul Sakuma/AP Images; **36:** wanpatsorn/Shutterstock; **42:** Jesus Sanz/Shutterstock; **45:** Redpixel.PL/Shutterstock; **52:** Shutterstock; **63:** IVASHstudio/Shutterstock; **67:** Courtesy of Tom Kraemer and Bob Pagani; **70:** John Zich/AFP/Getty Images; **72:** Herschel Hoffmeyer/Shutterstock; **75:** Nolan777/123RF; **76:** *(tl)* Paleontologist natural/Shutterstock, *(tr)* Filipao Photography/Shutterstock, *(bl)* Luke. Travel/Shutterstock, *(br)* DejaVuDesigns/Shutterstock; **78:** ImageFlow/Shutterstock; **86:** *(t, b)* Courtesy of West Virginia Division of Culture and History; **87:** *(l, r)* Courtesy of West Virginia Division of Culture and History; **88:** Courtesy of West Virginia Division of Culture and History; **96:** Richard Cavalleri/Shutterstock; **99:** Armanita/Shutterstock; **101:** Witthaya Prasongsin/123RF; **102:** Quietbits/Shutterstock; **104:** Worradirek/Shutterstock; **109:** hidesy/Shutterstock; **116:** Jeoffrey Maitem/Getty Images News/Getty Images; **118:** *(birds)* Alexey Khromushin/Shutterstock, *(medal)* Natale Matteo/Shutterstock; **129:** *(t)* Worldwide Features/Barcroft Media/Getty Images, *(b)* John Ewin/Portland Press Herald/Getty Images; **130:** Steve Kagan/The LIFE Images Collection/Getty Images.

TEXT CREDITS

Pages 9–10: Based on Zorba Paster and Susan Meltsner: *The Longevity Code*, copyright © 2001 by Zorba Paster.

25–26: From *Let Your Life Speak*, Parker Palmer, copyright © 1999. Reprinted with permission of John Wiley and Sons, Inc.

41–42: Based on Jon Katz, *Geeks*, copyright © 2000 by Jon Katz.

53–54: Adapted from Jeff Maysh "A Catfishing with a Happy Ending," The Atlantic, October 17, 2017. https://www.theatlantic.com/technology/archive/2017/10/hooklineandsinker/542748/. Used with permission.

60: From Hayley Kaufman "Marriage, 20-Something Style," *Boston Globe*, 24 June 2001. Copyright © by The Boston Globe. Reprinted by permission of the Boston Globe via the Copyright Clearance Center.

93–94: Excerpted from "The Neighbors from Hell" by Mark Stuart Gill, Copyright June 1994, Meredith Corporation. All rights reserved. Used with the permission of *Ladies Home Journal.*

109–110: The Chicks' four rules are reprinted by permission of International Creative Management, Inc. Copyright © 2001 by Karin Housely.

128: The statistics in the graph are from the research of P. Amato (1993) "Helping behavior in urban and rural environments." *Journal of Personality and Social Psychology*, 45: 571–586.

3. Neighbors tried for 15 years to get the woman to clean up her yard. Finally, the neighbors decided to sue her for the emotional harm looking at the junk was causing them. The judge awarded the neighbors $114,000. The woman refused to pay and was sentenced to 30 days in jail. She disappeared, and the city sold her house. The new owners found two to three feet of trash in every room and piles of garbage on every bed.
4. Neighbors complained to their city's planning commission. The planning commission asked the billionaire to meet with his neighbors and a mediator. The billionaire promised to limit construction hours and complete the house within one year.
5. The problem with the parrot was never really resolved. The neighbors complained at City Hall, and an official there found a law that forbids anyone from "allowing any animal or bird to make loud noises." The city asked Bubba's owner to keep Bubba inside. She refused. The feud between Bubba's owner and the neighbors continued for two years. Finally, the neighbors who complained the most about Bubba moved. Bubba is still on the balcony and has become a TV star.

UNIT 7

PRE-READING page 102

1. **Statue of the bull:** The sculptor, Arturo Di Modica, says the bull "celebrates the can-do spirit of America and especially New York, where people from all over the world could come regardless of their origin or circumstances." A "bull market" means that stock prices are rising, so to many people the bull represents prosperity and optimism about the stock market.

   Statue of the girl: The sculpture is called "Fearless Girl." Its sculptor, Kristen Visbal, says the girl is "brave, proud, and strong." This work of art is meant to encourage companies to put more women in positions of leadership.

CONTENTS

continued ▶

CONTENTS (continued)

INTRODUCTION

TRUE STORIES, SILVER EDITION

The Silver Edition of *True Stories* is a five-level reading series. The series is appropriate for low-beginning to high-intermediate learners of English as a Second or Foreign Language. The Silver Edition consists of revised editions of six of the highly successful and popular *True Stories in the News* books that have provided entertaining stories and effective reading skill instruction for many years. In fact, the first book in that series was published over twenty-five years ago (hence the title "Silver" Edition). The *True Stories* series has been going strong ever since.

NEW IN THE SILVER EDITION

- **New and updated stories.** Some stories have been updated, and some have been replaced with fresh new readings that have been thoroughly classroom-tested before making it into print. All of the readings that have proven to be favorites of students and teachers over the years have been retained.
- **A colorful new design.** Originally published solely in black and white, the new edition has a new full-color design with colorful new photos. The color design makes the readings even more inviting, and the color photos that accompany the readings enhance understanding and enjoyment of the stories.
- **A uniform unit structure.** The books in the series have been given a consistent unit structure that runs across all six books. This predictable structure makes it easy for teachers to teach the series at different levels and for students to progress seamlessly from one level to the next.
- **Audio recordings of every reading.** Every story in the series has been recorded and made available online for students or teachers to download. (In Level 5, only the first reading—the True Story in the News—has been recorded.)
- **Online Answer Keys and To the Teacher notes.** The Answer Keys are now online as downloadable pdfs. Teachers may provide these to the students should they wish. Additional practice activities are also now available online.

THE APPROACH

The underlying premise in this series has always been that when second language learners are engaged in a pleasurable reading experience in the second language, then language learning will take place effortlessly and effectively. The formula is simple: Offer students a true story that fascinates and surprises them. Have them read and enjoy the story. Focus their attention on some useful vocabulary in the story. Confirm that they fully understand the story with reading comprehension exercises. Develop reading skills that progress from basic to more complex. Finally, use the content and the topic of the story to engage in discussion and writing tasks, from tightly structured to more open-ended.

UNIT COMPONENTS

Pre-Reading

Each unit begins with a pre-reading task that piques students' curiosity about the content of the story. Students' attention is drawn to the art that accompanies the reading and the title of the reading as they predict what the story is going to be about.

Reading

The readings are short enough to be read by the students in class; at the lower levels, the stories can be read in minutes. As the levels become higher, the readings do become longer and more challenging. Still, even at the highest levels, each reading and the exercises immediately following it can be completed in one class meeting.

Post-Reading

While there is some variation in the post-reading activities, the following are in all six books:

- **Vocabulary.** Useful key vocabulary items are selected from the readings for presentation and practice. The vocabulary activities vary from unit to unit, and the number of vocabulary items and the extent of the practice increases from level to level.
- **Comprehension.** At least two different comprehension tasks follow the vocabulary section. The exercises have descriptive titles, such as Understanding the Main Ideas, Remembering Details, or Understanding Cause and Effect, so that teachers and students know which cognitive skills are being applied. The exercises have a great deal of variety, keeping students engaged and motivated.
- **Discussion.** Having read and studied the stories, students are encouraged to discuss some aspect arising from the story. Even at the lowest level, students are given simple tasks that will give them the opportunity to talk in pairs, in small groups, or as a whole class.
- **Writing.** The final section of each unit has students produce a short piece of writing related to the reading. Often the writing task derives directly from the Discussion, in which case the title of the section is Discussion/Writing. The writing tasks are level-appropriate and vary in complexity depending on student proficiency. The tasks are not intended to be graded. They simply provide a final opportunity for students to engage with the topic of the reading and deepen their understanding and enjoyment of the story.

TRUE STORIES, LEVEL 5

True Stories, Level 5 is the highest level in the Silver Edition of the *True Stories* series. It is intended for high-intermediate learners of English. It consists of eight 14- to 18-page units, each with the following distinguishing features:

- ample discussion and writing exercises that make Level 5 well suited for integrated-skills courses, such as those that combine instruction in reading, writing, and speaking.
- a design that allows the unit to stand alone and be completed at any time.
- two reading selections that offer distinctly different reading experiences.

ACKNOWLEDGMENTS

I would like to thank

- the many teachers whose invaluable feedback helped me assess how the stories and exercises were working outside the small sphere of my own classroom. If I were to list you all by name, this acknowledgments section would go on for pages. I would like to thank three colleagues in particular: legendary teacher Peggy Miles, who introduced me to the world of English language teaching; Sharron Bassano, whose innovative techniques for teaching beginning-level students informed my own approach; and Jorge Islas Martinez, whose enthusiasm and dedication remain a constant inspiration;
- my students, who shared personal stories that became the examples for the discussion and writing exercises;
- the people in the stories who supplied details that were not in news sources: Twyla Thompson, John Koehler, Dorothy Peckham, Chi Hsii Tsui, Margaret Patrick, Trish Moore and Rhonda Gill (grandmother and mother of Desiree), Friendship Force participants, Natalie Garibian, Mirsada Buric, and the late Irvin Scott;
- the teachers and editors who made important contributions at different stages of development to the previous editions of these books and whose influence can still be seen throughout this new edition: Allen Ascher, John Barnes, Karen Davy, Joanne Dresner, Nancy Hayward, Stacey Hunter, Penny LaPorte, Laura LeDrean, Françoise Leffler, Linda Moser, Dana Klinek Pinter, Mary Perrotta Rich, Debbie Sistino, and Paula Van Ells;
- Rachel Hayward and Megan Hohenstein, who assisted in piloting and researching new material for the Silver Edition;
- the team at Pearson, whose experienced hands skillfully put together all the moving pieces in the preparation of this Silver Edition: Pietro Alongi, Tracey Cataldo, Warren Fischbach, Lucy Hart, Gosia Jaros-White, Linda Moser, Dana Pinter, Joseph Vella, and Peter West;
- copyeditor and fact checker, Kate Smyres; and proofreader, Ann Dickson;
- editor extraordinaire Françoise Leffler, who lent her expertise to *True Stories* levels 4 and 5;
- Bernard Seal at Page Designs International, who guided this project from start to finish with dedication, creativity, pragmatism, and the occasional "crazy"—but brilliant—idea;
- Don Williams at Page Designs International, whose talent for design is evident on every page; and
- my husband, John Hajdu Heyer, who read the first draft of every story I've considered for the *True Stories* series. The expression on his face as he read told me whether or not the story was a keeper. He didn't know that. Now he does.

FROM THE AUTHOR

Dear Teachers and Students,

This new edition of *True Stories* is the Silver Edition because it celebrates an anniversary—it has been more than 25 years since the first *True Stories* book was published. The way we get our news has changed a lot over the years, but some things have remained the same: Fascinating stories are in the news every day, and the goal of the *True Stories* series is still to bring the best of them to you.

The question students ask most often about these stories is *Are they true?* The answer is *yes*—to the best of my knowledge, these stories are true. I've fact-checked stories by contacting reporters, photojournalists, and research librarians all over the world. I've even called some of the people in the stories to be sure I have the facts right.

Once I'm as sure as I can be that a story is true, the story has to pass one more test. My students read the story, and after they finish reading, they give each story one, two, or three stars. They take this responsibility seriously; they know that only the top-rated stories will become part of the *True Stories* reading series.

I hope that you, too, think these are three-star stories. And I hope that reading them encourages you to share your own stories, which are always the most amazing true stories of all.

Sandra Heyer

UNIT 1

Longevity

The theme of this unit is longevity—a long life. How long is "a long life"? How old is "old"? Are you old when you turn 50...or 60...or 75...or 80?

A **Think about this question. Write a number on the line. Then read your number aloud and listen as your classmates read their numbers aloud.**

In your opinion, at what age does a person become "old"? ________

B **Discuss the answers to these questions with your classmates.**

1. Why did you write the number you did? Why do you think someone becomes old at that age?
2. Do your classmates agree on what is old? That is, did most people write numbers that are close to one another? If there is a big difference between the lowest number and the highest number, what could explain the difference?
3. Can you notice any patterns in the numbers people chose? For example, did older classmates write higher numbers than younger classmates? Did classmates from the same part of the world write numbers that are close to one another?

In this unit, you will read about some people who are very old. First, you will read about a village in Italy where people often live to be 90, and even older. Then you will read a doctor's advice on how *you* can have a long, sweet life.

A TRUE STORY IN THE NEWS

PRE-READING

The man in the photo is very old. Yet he still enjoys working in the fields—and he rides his bike to work! That would surprise some people, but not someone who lives in Campodimele, Italy. Campodimele is a village in Italy where most people stay healthy and busy well into their 90s.

A **With your classmates, make a list of possible reasons people stay healthy and live long in Campodimele.**

B **Read the story to find out what researchers concluded.**

La Dolce Vita (The Sweet Life)

1 When he was 34 years old, Gerardo Pecchia left his village in Italy to work in the United States. He worked in the United States for 40 years; then, at the age of 74, he retired and returned to Campodimele, his native village.

2 Campodimele was as beautiful as Gerardo remembered it. The tiny town is on a mountain-top 75 miles (120 kilometers) south of Rome, surrounded by olive trees. A medieval wall encircles the village, and narrow stone streets wind between its quaint old houses. In the center of the town there is a picturesque *piazza*—a town square—where people gather to chat in the shade of a 300-year old elm tree. Even the weather in Campodimele is beautiful: At 2,100 feet (650 meters) above sea level, the town catches fresh sea breezes that keep the temperatures moderate—not too hot and not too cold.

3 Gerardo was happy to be back in Campodimele among family and old friends. He was happy, too, that he had enough money to enjoy his retirement. During his 40 years in the United States, he had paid into the Social Security fund, so he received a small pension. Each time he cashed a check, he exchanged his U.S. dollars for Italian lira, and he had enough lira to live a simple but comfortable life.

4 Gerardo lived contentedly in Campodimele for 25 years; then, when he was 99 years old, he had a serious problem—not with his health, as could be expected at that age—but with the U.S. government. Officials at the U.S. Embassy in Rome noticed that a 99-year-old man named Gerardo Pecchia was cashing Social Security checks in Campodimele. They had a hard time believing that Gerardo Pecchia could still be alive. Perhaps he had died, they thought, and a son or nephew with the same name was illegally cashing the checks. Embassy officials wrote Mr. Pecchia, asking for proof that he was alive. Gerardo traveled to Rome and went to the embassy in person. "I am Gerardo Pecchia," he told the officials there. "As you can see, I am still alive."

5 Gerardo Pecchia was not just alive—he was alive and well. He was still taking care of his garden, still doing his own shopping, still taking the bus to visit his son. Anywhere else in the world, people would be amazed to see a 99-year-old man with such vitality. In Campodimele, however, it is not a surprising sight. In the tiny town of 890 people, 48 are over the age of 90, and most of them, like Gerardo, are healthy and busy. They chop wood, milk cows, and hunt; they take care of gardens and olive trees. One 94-year-old man is often seen riding his bright blue moped on the mountainous roads around Campodimele.

6 When Gerardo retired in Campodimele, he retired in one of the healthiest places on earth. It is rare for anybody in Campodimele to die before reaching the age of 85, and people remain healthy and active well into their 90s. In 1985, the World Health Organization sent a team of medical researchers to Campodimele. Their task was to determine why people there lived such long and healthy lives. The researchers discovered that the blood pressure of elderly Campodimeleans was exceptionally low. It was not unusual for a 90-year-old man to have the same blood pressure level as his 20-year-old great-grandson. Cholesterol levels were low, too—around 100, less than half the usual level in most Western nations. These findings fascinated the researchers. If Campodimeleans can have such low blood pressure and cholesterol levels, why can't we all? What is their secret? Is it diet? Is it lifestyle? Or is it simply good genes?

7 Some residents of Campodimele credit the water they drink for their longevity and health. For centuries the village has been known for its mineral water, which people collect from several fountains in the town. People claim the minerals in the water prevent hardening of the arteries. Other residents credit the food they eat for their good health. The people of Campodimele eat a traditional Mediterranean diet, which consists mainly of fresh vegetables, pasta, wild mushrooms, olive oil, shallots, and a moderate amount of red wine. They eat very

continued ▶

little meat, salt, or butter, and very few people in the village are heavy coffee drinkers, unlike other Italians. A typical lunch in Campodimele might be homemade bread grilled with olive oil and tomatoes; spaghetti with carrots, onions, and tomatoes; and perhaps some seafood, snails fried in olive oil, or local beans called *cicerchie*.

8 The researchers wondered if the lifestyle in Campodimele could be having a positive effect on residents' health, so they observed people as they went about their daily lives. The researchers concluded that the lifestyle did have a positive effect. In Campodimele, most people follow a traditional rural timetable: They get up at sunrise, go to bed at 8 p.m., and eat at the same time every day. They also get plenty of exercise. Because the streets are so narrow, walking is the usual way to get around Campodimele. Nearly everyone works daily in gardens or takes care of chickens or other small animals. Many of Campodimele's inhabitants are farmers, and they keep fit walking up and down the steep hillside that separates the village from their plots of land. In addition, the lifestyle seems, at least on the surface, to be free of stress. There is no crime in Campodimele, and there is no traffic because cars are not allowed in the center of the village. Perhaps most important, elderly people are not separated from younger people; they do not live in retirement homes, but instead are well integrated with the rest of the population. In Campodimele, it is not unusual to see four generations gather to chat under the elm tree in the piazza. Dr. Pietro Cugini, who led the research, noted: "The elderly person is never alone, but has a life synchronized with that of others, as in one big family."

9 In addition to examining the water, diet, and lifestyle in Campodimele, the researchers tried to determine if the longevity of Campodimeleans, who have been members of only a few families for centuries, has a genetic cause. Dr. Cugini believes that genes do play a role. Many inhabitants have a special enzyme that reduces blood pressure and cholesterol levels. Moreover, a study of Campodimeleans who left the village for Toronto, Canada, in the 1960s showed that they, too, lived long and healthy lives—an indication that Campodimeleans carry a gene for longevity. Still, Dr. Cugini does not think that good genes alone guarantee longevity. "You also need a well-structured lifestyle," he warns. At the end of the four-year study, he concluded that the villagers' health and longevity are based 30 percent on genetics and 70 percent on environment.

10 The old people in Campodimele seemed puzzled by all the laboratory tests and record-keeping. Pasquale Pannozzi, 83, wondered, "I don't know why they are spending all this time in Campodimele. The answer is easy: This is a perfect spot. No stress. Who would want to die?"

Hills near Campodimele

GETTING THE BIG PICTURE

Why do the people of Campodimele have unusually long and healthy lives? Circle the letter of your answer.

a. They have a healthy diet, a healthy lifestyle, and good genes. The fact that Campodimele is beautiful—"a perfect spot"—probably helps, too.

b. Fresh sea breezes keep the air clean. Although the town is only 75 miles from Rome, there is no pollution.

c. Doctors from the World Health Organization have been living in Campodimele since 1985, studying the people. Campodimeleans have the best medical care in the world.

BUILDING VOCABULARY

RECALLING NEW WORDS

The words below are from the story. Complete each sentence with the correct word or words.

amazed	pension	retire	wind *(verb)*
had a hard time	proof	rural	
native village	puzzled	vitality	

1. Gerardo Pecchia was born in a small town in Italy, but he went to the United States when he was 34. Forty years later, he returned to his native village.
2. Most people stop working when they are 65, but Gerardo didn't ____________ until he was 74.
3. Gerardo paid taxes when he worked in the United States, so when he retired, he received a little money every month from the U.S. government. His ____________ was small, but he had enough money to live comfortably.
4. It was difficult for the embassy officials to believe that a 99-year-old man was still cashing Social Security checks. They ____________ believing that Mr. Pecchia was still alive.
5. Embassy officials wanted Mr. Pecchia to show them that he was still living: They wanted to see papers or other information. They wanted ____________ that he was alive.
6. Gerardo had a lot of energy: He was taking care of his garden, doing his own shopping, and taking the bus to visit his son. Like many old people in Campodimele, he had great ____________.
7. In Campodimele, people are not surprised when they see 90-year-olds hunting and chopping wood. In other places in the world, however, people would be so surprised, they would find it hard to believe. They would be ____________ to see it.

8. Campodimele sits on the top of a mountain, so its streets cannot be straight. They go around the mountain and ____________________ between the houses.

9. Many of the people in Campodimele are farmers, and almost everyone has a garden or small animals. Campodimele is in a ____________________ part of Italy.

10. The old people in Campodimele didn't understand why the researchers wanted to study them. They were ____________________ by all the laboratory tests and record-keeping.

USING CONTEXT CLUES

Sometimes you can find the meaning of a word or phrase from the context clues—the surrounding words and sentences. Before looking up a word in a dictionary, check for context clues.

In each sentence, circle the word or words that have the same meaning as the words in *italics*. The first one is done for you.

1. In the center of the town, there is a *piazza*—a town square—where people gather.
2. Campodimele has *moderate temperatures*—not too hot and not too cold.
3. Gerardo was happy and satisfied because his life was good in Campodimele. He was *contented* there.
4. A typical lunch in Campodimele might be homemade bread; spaghetti with carrots, onions, and tomatoes; and perhaps some seafood, snails fried in olive oil, or local beans called *cicerchie*.
5. In Italy, there are people who drink a lot of coffee, but the people in Campodimele are not *heavy coffee drinkers*.
6. The researchers wondered if the lifestyle in Campodimele could be having a positive effect on *residents'* health, so they observed the people living there as they went about their daily lives.
7. Elderly people are not separated from younger people; they are well *integrated* with the rest of the population.
8. Researchers wondered if genes have an influence on Campodimeleans' longevity. They discovered that genes do *play a role*.

DEVELOPING READING SKILLS

UNDERSTANDING THE MAIN IDEAS

There are three correct ways to complete each sentence. Cross out the one incorrect answer.

1. Campodimele
   a. is a tiny town on a mountaintop 75 miles from Rome.
   b. ~~was the birthplace of many famous Italians.~~
   c. is a beautiful town that has beautiful weather.
   d. is one of the healthiest places on earth.

2. The people of Campodimele
   a. rarely die before age 85.
   b. travel to Canada for medical care.
   c. remain healthy and active well into their 90s.
   d. have low blood pressure and low cholesterol levels.

3. The medical researchers who went to Campodimele
   a. were sent by the World Health Organization.
   b. tried to determine why people in Campodimele lived such long and healthy lives.
   c. observed people as they went about their daily lives.
   d. concluded that the lifestyle in Campodimele did not have a positive effect on residents' health.

4. The doctor who led the research in Campodimele
   a. noticed that elderly people are never alone.
   b. believes that good genes guarantee longevity.
   c. believes people need a well-structured lifestyle.
   d. concluded that Campodimeleans' health and longevity are based 30 percent on genetics and 70 percent on environment.

UNDERSTANDING SUPPORTING IDEAS

The ability to understand which information supports a main idea is an important reading skill. Sentences with supporting ideas give you more information about the main ideas, often by explaining or giving examples. For example, look at paragraph 2 of "*La Dolce Vita*" on page 3. The main idea of the paragraph—that Campodimele is beautiful—is followed by many supporting ideas: "The tiny town is…surrounded by olive trees…narrow stone streets wind between its quaint old houses. In the center of the town there is a picturesque *piazza*—a town square…"

Read each sentence below. Then write a sentence that gives more information.

1. Gerardo Pecchia was alive and well. He was still taking care of his garden, still doing his own shopping, and still taking the bus to visit his son.

2. Some Campodimeleans credit the water they drink for their longevity. They believe it contains minerals which prevents hardening of the arteries.

3. Campodimeleans eat a traditional Mediterranean diet. ______

4. Most people follow a traditional rural timetable. ______

5. Campodimeleans get plenty of exercise. ______

6. The lifestyle seems free of stress. ______

UNDERSTANDING AN IDEA MAP

An *idea map* presents the main ideas and the supporting ideas of a reading in a visual way. Drawing an idea map after you read helps you recognize how a reading is organized and helps you remember the main ideas.

Look at the idea map below, which represents the organization of the story "*La Dolce Vita*." Some information is missing from the map. Write the missing information on each line.

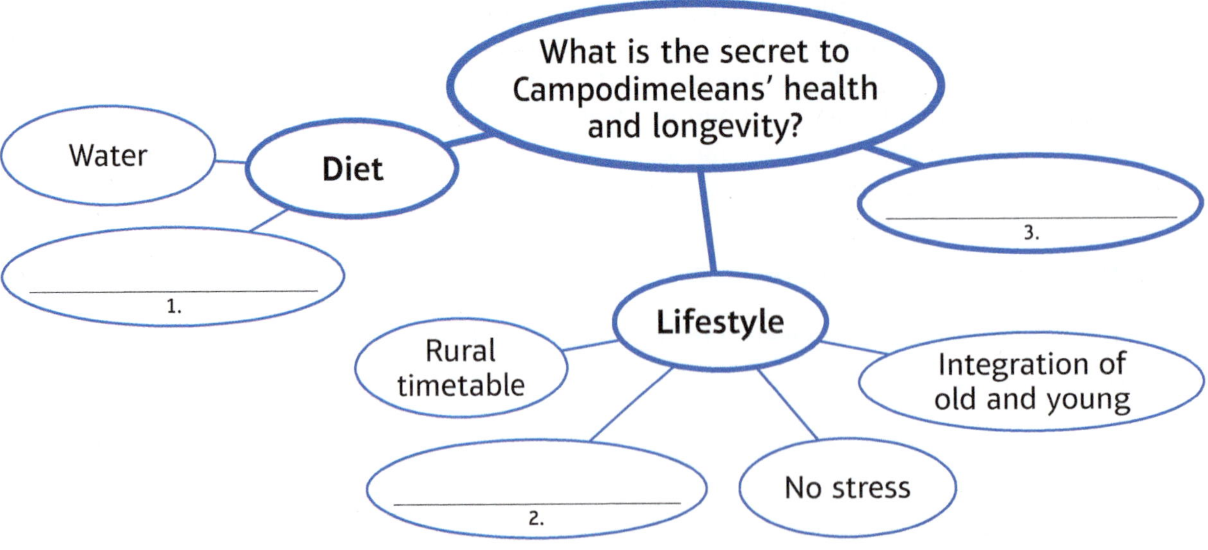

NEWS AND VIEWS

How can we have long and healthy lives like the people of Campodimele, Italy? Dr. Zorba Paster has some suggestions.

Dr. Paster is a medical doctor and a professor at the University of Wisconsin Medical School. He gives medical advice on a weekly radio show and has written a book called *The Longevity Code*. In his book, Dr. Paster tells us how to have long, healthy lives. His advice is based on scientific research, his own experience as a doctor, and common sense. Here is a summary of his "prescription" for a long, sweet life.

Before you begin reading, look at the six subheadings. Each subheading gives you the topic of the paragraphs below it. Notice, too, the illustration of the five interlocking rings. What could be the connection between the rings and the topic of the article—how to have a long, healthy life? (Take a guess, and remember that no logical guess is wrong.)

The Longevity Code by Dr. Zorba Paster

1 Jeanne Calment, of Arles, France, was still riding her bicycle at age 100. And at age 110, she was still living in her own apartment. When she died in 1997 at the age of 122, she had lived longer than any person on record.

2 Perhaps you wouldn't want to live to 122, but certainly you would like to live a long and healthy life. We all want to know the tricks for prolonging our lives, and physicians and researchers have written thousands of pages on the topic. Most of them write about the benefits of taking care of your body: Cut your cholesterol, lose weight, exercise, stop smoking, and watch your blood pressure. While cholesterol, diet, exercise, and not smoking are important, there is more to consider. Just as critical are how much you like your job, whether you have a good relationship with your parents and children, whether you're depressed or happy, angry or delighted, mean or kindhearted.

3 We would all agree that these factors count in quality of life. The fact is that they count in length of life, too—perhaps even as much as the physical factors your doctor can treat. The truth is that being well does not simply mean being in great physical shape. Overall good health is composed of five unique spheres of wellness: the physical, the mental, the family and social, the spiritual, and the material. Picture the Olympic symbol of five interlocking rings. Like the Olympic rings, the five spheres of wellness overlap and interact. Most of us have experienced the way the spheres affect one another. Perhaps mental stress caused a headache, which hurt so much you stayed home from a party, which meant you spent Saturday night alone, which made you so depressed you ate a quart of ice cream. Or perhaps the spheres of wellness interacted in a positive way: A peaceful walk on the beach calmed your mind, relaxed your body, gave you physical exercise, helped you sleep better, made you more pleasant to be around, and so on.

4 In order to live a life that is not only long, but happy, satisfied, and fulfilling—what Dr. Paster calls a "sweet" life—you must have good health in all five spheres. Knowing which areas need the most improvement and which are already healthy is the key to increasing your life span.

Sphere #1: Physical

5 There is more to physical health than being "healthy"—that is, not being sick. To increase your chances of having a long life, you also need to pay attention to physical fitness,

continued ▶

nutrition, and safety strategies, like wearing a seat belt.

6 Physical fitness is definitely a plus in the physical sphere. Basically, the secret to physical fitness is being active. The more we use our muscles—whether we use them to clean the house or run a marathon—the more physically fit, energetic, and long-lived we're likely to be. Sedentary lifestyles, on the other hand, limit longevity—they're one of the top ten causes of premature death.

Sphere #2: Mental

7 There are a number of psychological illnesses that have a negative impact on longevity. Depression is one of them; severe anxiety is another. So, if you are depressed or very anxious, it's important to find the treatment that will help you.

8 It's also important to control your anger. Becoming furious over every small frustration is truly deadly: Studies indicate that after a fit of anger—especially the face-reddening, fist-clenching, furniture-pounding kind—the risk of having a heart attack is more than twice as high.

9 Finally, it's important to keep your mind sharp and challenged. Lifelong learning is one way to do that. As we age, one of our greatest fears is that our bodies will keep going but our minds will stop working. Lifelong learning keeps our minds active.

Sphere #3: Family and Social

10 A recent study compared the longevity of three groups of people: "couch potatoes" (sedentary types who spent most of their free time watching TV), "gym rats" (people who were compulsive about exercising), and "social butterflies" (people who often got together with other people). Guess which group had the longest and healthiest lives? The social butterflies.

11 Bonds with other people improve our outlook and build self-confidence. Social support also helps us get through stressful times. Those of us who have the support of family and friends are less likely to have heart disease and generally live longer.

Sphere #4: Spiritual

12 Physicians rarely talk about religion; it's a topic that's so personal, it's almost taboo. Yet scientific evidence shows that a spiritual or religious path not only gives comfort but also adds to longevity.

13 The spiritual sphere is the most difficult to describe. It includes anything we do to contemplate the higher meaning and purpose of our lives: meditation, prayer, attending religious services, reading inspirational material, chanting, sitting quietly in a garden, or walking through a forest. And yes, all of this affects life expectancy and life quality.

Sphere #5: Material

14 The material sphere is where you find all your "stuff"—all the things outside yourself that affect how you feel. This sphere includes your job, your house, your car, your bank account, and your credit card debt.

15 One part of the material sphere is financial. Having a lot of money is not important, but being content with what you have is. A huge home, luxury cars, and diamonds will not make your life better or help you live longer. However, if not having those things makes you feel ashamed or jealous, then not having what you want could be a problem. Indeed, simply feeling that you don't have enough can shorten your life.

Creating Balance

16 Diet, exercise, and quitting smoking are important, but they are not the only keys to having a long and healthy life. Meditating might also be important, or planting a garden, or playing cards with friends. If those things calm and relax you, bring you pleasure or make you laugh, then do them.

17 Longevity is a two-sided coin, with quantity on one side and quality on the other. Just as no one wants a great life that's cut short prematurely, no one wants a life that's long but not satisfying. We want to have it both ways—long *and* great. In fact, we can have long, great lives when we balance the five spheres of wellness.

BUILDING ACADEMIC VOCABULARY

The words below are on the Academic Word List.* Find the words in *The Longevity Code*. (The number in parentheses is the number of the paragraph.) If you are not sure what a word means, look it up in your dictionary. Then use the words in the sentences that follow.

topic (2, 12)	interact (3)	definitely (6)	evidence (12)
overall (3)	positive (3)	impact (7)	
overlap (3)	physical (5)	challenge (9)	

1. Many scientists say that climate change could have a big ____impact____ on the lives of people who live in coastal areas.
2. He is working as a gardener because he would rather be outside doing ____________________ work than inside doing mental work.
3. Don't drink citrus juice when you take this medicine. The citric acid in the juice will ____________________ with the medicine, and the medicine won't work.
4. Both the advertising and marketing departments have a common goal: They want as many people as possible to know about the company's products. As a result, the responsibilities of the two departments ____________________ somewhat.
5. Because she is taking five difficult classes this semester, getting good grades is a ____________________.
6. Doctors say that eating a lot of fruit and vegetables has a ____________________ effect on your health.
7. This evening, environmentalists are going to talk about cleaning up our polluted rivers. I'm going to their presentation because I'm interested in the ____________________.
8. His teacher told him he might get a B as his final grade, or maybe a B+, but ____________________ not an A.
9. We had some bad weather on our vacation. But we had great food, met interesting people, and visited beautiful places. So ____________________ it was a good trip.
10. Police were quite certain he had committed the crime, but they did not arrest him because they had no ____________________.

* This is a list of over 500 words commonly found in textbooks written in English. The list was created by Dr. Avril Coxhead of Victoria University, New Zealand. You can find the complete list online by searching "Academic Word List."

DEVELOPING READING SKILLS

UNDERSTANDING THE MAIN IDEAS

According to Dr. Paster, what is the best way to increase your chances of having a long and healthy life? Circle the letter of your answer.

a. Take care of your body: Cut your cholesterol, lose weight, exercise, stop smoking, and watch your blood pressure. Research shows that taking care of your body has great benefits.

b. Be sure you have health in all five spheres of your life—the physical, mental, family/social, spiritual, and material—because these five spheres overlap and interact.

c. Examine the five spheres of your life—the physical, mental, family/social, spiritual, and material—and decide which sphere is most important to you. Good health in this sphere is critical.

RECOGNIZING SUPPORTING EVIDENCE

> To convince us that they are correct, writers sometimes support their statements with evidence. Being able to recognize supporting evidence can help you become a better reader.

Read the sentences that state Dr. Paster's advice. Match each statement with the scientific evidence that Dr. Paster gives to support it. Write the letter of your answer on the line.

Advice

__e__ 1. Be content with what you have.

_____ 2. Have bonds with other people.

_____ 3. Contemplate the meaning and purpose of your life, perhaps by sitting quietly in a garden or by walking in a forest.

_____ 4. Be active, whether you use your muscles to run a marathon or to clean the house.

_____ 5. Try not to become furious over every small frustration.

Evidence

a. Sedentary lifestyles are one of the top ten causes of premature death.

b. Studies indicate that a fit of anger doubles your risk of having a heart attack.

c. A recent study comparing the longevity of three groups of people—couch potatoes, gym rats, and social butterflies—showed that the social butterflies had the longest and healthiest lives.

d. Scientific evidence shows that a spiritual or religious path adds to longevity.

e. Feeling that you don't have enough money can shorten your life.

APPLYING INFORMATION

Look at the photos. Are the people in each photo following Dr. Paster's advice for a long, sweet life or not? What makes you think so? Write your answer on a piece of paper.

Example:

The women in the first photo appear to be friends, and Dr. Paster says that bonds with other people help us live longer. So, they are following Dr. Paster's advice. But maybe they can't buy the clothes they're looking at because they don't have enough money. If not having things makes them ashamed or jealous, it could shorten their lives.

READING A CHART

A **In the chart below, you will find the life-expectancy figures for men and women in 16 countries. Look at the list of countries without looking at the figures. (Cover them with a piece of paper.) Discuss the answers to these questions with your classmates.**

1. In which countries do you think people have the longest lives?
2. In which countries do you think people have the shortest lives?

Average Life Expectancies in Selected Countries

Country	Males	Females	Average
Brazil	71	78	74
Canada	79	85	82
China	74	78	76
Germany	79	83	81
Italy	80	85	82
Japan	82	89	85
Mexico	73	79	76
Nigeria	53	55	54
Pakistan	66	70	68
Poland	74	82	78
Russia	65	77	71
Saudi Arabia	73	78	76
Somalia	51	55	53
South Korea	79	86	83
Turkey	73	78	75
United States	78	82	80

B **Now use the chart to answer the following questions.**

1. Of all 16 countries, where do people live the longest? Did you guess correctly?
2. Where do people have the shortest lives? Did you guess correctly?
3. How do you explain the differences in life-expectancy figures all over the world?
4. Do women live longer than men in every country on the list?

DISCUSSION

In his book, *The Longevity Code*, Dr. Zorba Paster lists 76 steps you can take to prolong your life. He rates the steps from one star to five stars. The steps with five stars are, in his opinion, very important and will dramatically improve your chances for a longer, sweeter life. The steps with fewer stars are less important. The chart to the right shows three steps from his list and their ratings.

Steps	Stars
Stay away from tobacco.	★★★★★
Eat breakfast.	★★★
Save money.	★★

A **In a small group, read each step in Dr. Paster's list and guess how many stars Dr. Paster gives that step. Draw one to five stars in the chart.**

Steps	Stars
1. Don't overdo alcohol.	☆☆☆☆☆
2. Don't use illegal drugs, like heroin or cocaine.	
3. Eat more fruits and vegetables—five to seven per day.	
4. Cut the amount of fat in your diet.	
5. Fasten seat belts.	
6. Develop skills for coping with stress.	
7. Get enough sleep.	
8. Take care of your teeth and gums.	
9. Have a sense of humor.	
10. Build good relationships with friends.	
11. Own a pet.	
12. Make your workplace fun.	

B **After you are done guessing, check the Key on page 131 to see if you are correct. Then discuss the answers to these questions.**

1. Do you agree with Dr. Paster's ratings?
2. Dr. Paster wrote his book primarily for people who live in the United States. Are there steps on the list that might not be important for people from other countries?

C **In a group of three, choose one of the following three descriptions of research on longevity. Read it silently, and summarize it for the other two people in your group. Then think about the questions below each description, and discuss your answers with your classmates.**

1. **Eat less, live longer.** U.S. government scientists have learned they can extend the lifespan of rats by cutting the amount of food they eat. In experiments at the National Institutes of Health, scientists gave rats very little food—much less than the rats would eat if nobody were watching—but the food had all the nutrients the rats needed. It's a

technique called undernutrition without malnutrition—that is, eating less but eating well. This kind of serious undernutrition dramatically extended the lifespans of the rats: A 30 percent cut in food extended the average lifespan by 30 percent. A more recent study of a small group of humans who ate 15 percent less than usual over two years indicates that eating less could also extend the lifespan of people.

- After learning about this research, would you consider eating much less than you do now?
- Do you think thin people live longer than heavier people? If you have a story that supports your answer, tell it.

2. **Don't worry, be happy.** Positive emotions may prolong life. A professor at the University of Kentucky studied essays written in the 1930s by a group of women who were in their early 20s at the time. He searched the essays for positive emotions, looking for key words such as *happy*, *joy*, *love*, *hopeful*, and *content*. Then he checked to see how long each woman had lived. He discovered that the women who had expressed more positive emotions lived as much as 10 years longer than those expressing fewer positive emotions. The professor believes his study shows that controlling negative feelings is important to leading a longer, healthier life.
   - Do you think people can actually control how they feel?
   - Do you think happy people live longer than unhappy people? If you have a story that supports your answer, tell it.
3. **Sweet tooth, long life.** A recent study indicates that people who eat sweets live one year longer than people who don't. Researchers at Harvard University studied the medical records of more than 7,000 men. They discovered that healthy men who ate candy a few times a month added a year to their lives, with some men in the candy-eating group living as long as 95 years. The researchers did not ask the men if the candy they ate was chocolate, but now they wish they had. The researchers suspect that chocolate—not just any kind of candy—extends lifespan. Chocolate is known to have health benefits; perhaps it improves longevity as well as health.
   - Do you think this research gives people a reason to eat more candy?
   - After learning about this study, would you consider eating more candy?

WRITING

Choose one of the following topics to write about.

1. A man in Campodimele described his village as "a perfect spot." Make a poster for a place in your country that is a perfect spot to live. Title your poster "Top Five Reasons to Live in ________," and write the reasons in a bulleted list. Include a photo of the place on your poster.
2. Interview someone who is old and healthy. Ask the person, "What is your secret for a long and healthy life?" Then report what you learned.
3. Who is the oldest person you have ever known? Explain who the person is (or was) and why you think the person has lived (or lived) a long time.
4. Do you agree with Dr. Paster's idea that health in all five spheres is equally important? Or do you think that one sphere is more important than the others? Explain your answer.
5. Have you ever experienced the way the five spheres interact? Write about your experience.

UNIT 2

Finding Work That Is Right for You

Have you decided on the work that is right for you? How do you know it's right for you? Below is a list of factors people consider when they are thinking about what kind of work they want to do.

A **Read each factor on the list and write the first job you think of. (For example, if you wanted to make a lot of money, what work would you do?)**

1. making a lot of money __________
2. helping other people __________
3. doing a job that requires physical strength __________
4. doing similar things every day __________
5. taking long vacations __________
6. interacting with the public every day __________
7. traveling for my job __________
8. being my own boss __________
9. having job security __________
10. being creative __________

B **Discuss the answers to these questions with your classmates.**

1. Read your completed list aloud and listen as your classmates read theirs. Did any of your classmates' answers surprise you? (For example, are there jobs that pay a lot of money in some countries but not in others?)
2. Are there any jobs on your list that you have done or are thinking about doing?
3. Of all the factors on the list, which one is most important to you in choosing work?

In this unit, you will read about a blind young woman who dropped out of college when she realized her passion was food and she wanted to be a chef. Then you will read the advice of a man who believes he knows the secret to finding work that is right for you.

A TRUE STORY IN THE NEWS

Laura Martinez

PRE-READING

Look at the photo and read the title of the story on the next page. Then think about these questions. Discuss your answers with your classmates.

1. The woman in the photo, Laura Martinez, is a chef. She thinks it is a great job. Is it? What do you think?
2. With your classmates, make a list of "great jobs." Write your list on the board. (You and your classmates do not have to agree on which jobs belong on the list.) Is "chef" on your list of great jobs?

The Chef

1 Have you ever cooked something that was burnt on the outside but raw in the middle? Have you ever grilled meat that was too rare, or too well done? Has a pot ever boiled over? Has a cake ever stuck to a pan? Have you ever made food that was too greasy, too spicy, or too salty? Cooking has its challenges!

2 Now imagine cooking with your eyes closed. Imagine that additional challenge. That is what cooking is like for Laura Martinez. She is a blind chef.

3 When Laura was one year old, she was diagnosed with cancerous tumors in both her eyes. Doctors succeeded in curing the cancer with drugs and radiation, but they couldn't save Laura's sight.

4 Incredibly, for most of her childhood, Laura didn't know that she was blind. Born in Mexico, she grew up in a house surrounded by big trees that she climbed with her cousins. Her family and friends always treated her normally, and she had no reason to think that she was disabled in any way. When she was nine years old, her family moved to the United States. It wasn't until the summer before middle school that her family told her that she was blind. Until then, she had assumed that everyone experienced the world the way she did—through sound, touch, smell, and taste. She was shocked to learn that there was a fifth sense—sight.

5 Laura was a good learner, and she did well in middle school and high school. After she graduated from high school, she left home to go to college. She planned to major in psychology and become a psychologist because she knew there were blind psychologists. But she dropped out of college after the first year. She didn't leave because of experiences she had in the college's classrooms. She left because of experiences she had in the college's cafeteria.

6 Every time Laura walked into the cafeteria, she noticed the smells first. She couldn't help but compare them to the smells in her mother's kitchen back home. She remembered especially the smell of *mole*, a Mexican sauce made with chili peppers, black pepper, cinnamon, and cumin. When her mother ground the spices for *mole*, Laura thought the kitchen smelled awesome—so different from the cafeteria, which she thought smelled weird. She thought, too, about the fresh ingredients her mother used in her cooking. She suspected that the ingredients in the cafeteria food didn't come fresh from gardens, markets, or farms—they came from bottles, cans, and boxes.

7 Sitting in the cafeteria, trying to eat meals she hated, Laura realized that food, not psychology, was her passion. She didn't want to be a psychologist. She wanted to be a chef.

8 Fortunately for Laura, there was a great culinary school, Le Cordon Bleu, in Chicago, just a few hours from her parents' home. Unfortunately for Laura, the school was not interested in having her as a student. She wondered if it was because she was blind.

9 Determined to get into the school, she made an appointment to talk to someone in the president's office. The man she talked to was sympathetic. "My mother is blind, too," he told Laura, "but I don't think she's capable of doing something like cooking at Le Cordon Bleu." Laura responded, "How do you know? Give me a chance. And if I'm not able to succeed here, I'll pick up my things and leave—you won't even have to kick me out." Laura was admitted to Le Cordon Bleu.

10 In her last year of culinary school, Laura had some extraordinary luck. A famous chef—the owner of one of Chicago's top restaurants—stopped by for a visit. He paused in his tour of the kitchen to watch Laura. She was cooking by smell, taste, and touch, even touching simmering liquids to make sure the temperature was right. He tasted a piece of chicken Laura had cooked and then said, "You're going to work for me, right?"

11 "That would be an honor," Laura replied.

12 After she graduated from culinary school, Laura started working at the restaurant. It was her dream job. "We were like family," she remembers. "No one ever said, 'You can't do

continued ▶

this because you can't see.'" For three years, she prepped, cleaned, chopped, and cooked alongside Chicago's best chefs. Then the restaurant owner died suddenly, and the restaurant closed. Laura was out of work.

13 For a chef with a diploma from Le Cordon Bleu and three years' experience at a top restaurant, finding work as a chef should have been easy. For Laura, it wasn't easy; in fact, it was impossible. Laura says, "I went to *many* job interviews, and no luck. Nobody cared who I worked with, what I did, or where I studied. They just saw that I was blind." Finally, she realized she had a choice: She could keep looking for a job, or she could abandon the job search and start working on her dream—opening her own restaurant. She decided to open her own restaurant. She already knew what she wanted on the menu, and she already had a name: La Diosa, which means "the goddess" in Spanish. All she needed was financing. That, it turned out, wouldn't be easy to find, either.

14 Through an Internet search, Laura found the name of a business adviser, and she cold-called him. He agreed to meet with her after she told him on the phone about her training and experience. She did not tell him she was blind.

15 The business adviser was surprised when Laura, wearing her white chef coat, walked into his office; he had never met a blind chef. He was impressed by Laura's background: She'd graduated from Le Cordon Bleu. She'd worked at a top restaurant. She didn't have a business plan, but she knew exactly what she wanted to do. The question was: Could he help her turn her idea into a business? He thought he could.

16 Laura and her business adviser got to work—writing a business plan, applying for grants and loans, and visiting possible locations for the restaurant. Finally, two years later, La Diosa opened for business, with Laura as its owner and chef and her husband, Maurilio, as her assistant. Laura describes the restaurant this way: "It's tiny—just five tables and some stools at the counter at the front window—but it's like my baby; it's a great responsibility, and I put the best of me in it." The restaurant has an open kitchen, so customers can see Laura, wearing dark sunglasses, prepare their food.

17 When La Diosa opened, Laura's business adviser notified the media, and local newspapers and TV stations covered the event. The media coverage brought in a lot of customers. Ultimately, though, the success of the restaurant will depend on Laura's skills as a chef. And that's just fine with her. "I'm known for being the blind chef," she says. "But I want people to look beyond that. When people eat at La Diosa, what I really want them to remember is the food."

18 In that respect, La Diosa is already a success. If you look up La Diosa on business review websites such as Yelp or Zagat, you will find a lot of five-star reviews. People use words like these to describe the food: *Delicious. Amazing. Extraordinary. Fabulous. Outstanding. Wonderful.* Laura is pleased, of course, by the positive reviews people write online. But she is even more pleased by what they don't write: Very few of the reviewers mention that the chef is blind.

GETTING THE BIG PICTURE

Laura Martinez dreamed of being the chef in her own restaurant. It wasn't easy for her to make her dream a reality. Why not? Check (✓) three reasons.

- ☐ 1. Her family wanted her to become a psychologist.
- ☐ 2. She was blind.
- ☐ 3. The cooking school she wanted to go to wasn't interested in having her as a student.
- ☐ 4. A famous chef didn't like her cooking.
- ☐ 5. She couldn't get the ingredients that her mother used in Mexico.
- ☐ 6. She couldn't get financing for her restaurant.

BUILDING VOCABULARY

RECALLING NEW WORDS

The words below are from the story. Complete each sentence with the correct word or words.

capable of	dropped out of	kick somebody out	outstanding
culinary	grants	loans	sympathetic
disabled	greasy	media coverage	wondered

1. Laura was blind, but she never believed she was ___disabled___ in any way.
2. Laura left college after one year. She ____________ college because she didn't want to study psychology.
3. Laura wanted to study cooking, so she applied to a ____________ school.
4. The man in the president's office understood Laura's situation because his mother was blind. Although he was ____________, he did not want to admit Laura to cooking school.
5. In her interview at Le Cordon Bleu, Laura said that if she was not successful, she would leave. The school would not have to ____________ her ____________.
6. In cooking school, Laura learned the correct way to use ingredients like oil so that her food was not too ____________.
7. In the restaurant's kitchen, Laura cleaned lettuce for salads, chopped vegetables, and cooked food. She was ____________ doing everything the other chefs did.
8. Laura got money from banks to buy things for her restaurant. Of course, she will have to pay back the ____________.
9. Laura also got ____________ from businesses and organizations. She will not have to pay that money back.

10. When Laura's restaurant opened, reporters interviewed her. Stories about the restaurant were in newspapers, on the radio, and on TV. The restaurant got a lot of ____________________.

11. "A blind chef?" people asked. "How is that possible?" They ____________________ how Laura could do things like chop food and use the stove and oven.

12. People on business review sites give Laura's restaurant five stars out of a possible five stars. They use words like "excellent" and "____________________" to describe the food.

USING NEW WORDS

A Give examples to show you understand the meanings of the new words. You do not need to write in complete sentences.

Name...

1. something you are capable of doing. ____________________
2. something you wish you were capable of doing. ____________________
3. something people learn how to make in culinary school. ____________________
4. a business you would start if you got a grant. ____________________
5. a reason some students drop out of school. ____________________
6. a reason some students are kicked out of school. ____________________
7. a food from your country that is often greasy. ____________________
8. a situation you wish would get more media coverage. ____________________
9. a situation that makes you feel sympathetic. ____________________
10. something you often wonder about. ____________________
11. something you think is outstanding. ____________________

B In a small group, take turns reading your answers aloud. Ask your classmates questions about their answers.

DEVELOPING READING SKILLS

UNDERSTANDING THE MAIN IDEAS

There are two correct ways to complete each sentence. Cross out the one incorrect answer.

1. Laura never thought she was disabled because
   a. her family and friends treated her normally.
   b. her family didn't tell her she was blind.
   c. ~~her teachers told her she could succeed at anything.~~
2. In the cafeteria at the college Laura attended, she
   a. met other students from Mexico.
   b. thought about her mother's kitchen back home.
   c. realized that she didn't want to be a psychologist.
3. A man at the culinary school
   a. was sympathetic because his mother was blind, too.
   b. said he would do everything he could to help Laura succeed.
   c. didn't think that blind people were capable of cooking there.
4. During Laura's last year of culinary school, a famous chef
   a. watched her cook.
   b. offered her a job at his restaurant.
   c. offered her free cooking lessons.
5. When Laura decided to open her own restaurant, she already had
   a. the financing.
   b. the name.
   c. the menu.
6. The business adviser was impressed because Laura had
   a. a diploma from a great culinary school.
   b. experience at a top restaurant.
   c. a complete business plan.
7. Laura and her business adviser
   a. interviewed Chicago's best chefs.
   b. applied for grants and loans.
   c. visited possible locations for the restaurant.
8. Laura's restaurant has
   a. just five tables.
   b. an open kitchen.
   c. a Spanish theme.
9. On business review sites for Laura's restaurant, you'll see
   a. five-star reviews.
   b. links to news articles about her.
   c. words that describe the food.

RECOGNIZING CONTRASTING IDEAS

Words like *but, though,* and *or* are often used to connect contrasting ideas in writing. Punctuation marks like semicolons (;) and dashes (–) can be used in this way, too.

Complete the sentences with contrasting ideas from the story. Notice the words and punctuation that connect the contrasting ideas.

1. Have you ever cooked food that was burnt on the outside but raw in the middle ______?
2. Have you ever grilled meat that was too rare or too ______?
3. Laura thought her mother's kitchen smelled awesome—so different from the cafeteria, which she thought smelled ______.
4. The cafeteria food didn't come from gardens, markets, or farms—it came from ______.
5. For Laura, finding work as a chef wasn't easy; in fact, it was ______.
6. Laura could keep looking for a job as a chef, or she could ______.
7. Laura told a business adviser on the phone about her training and experience, but she didn't tell him ______.
8. The media coverage brought in a lot of customers. Ultimately, though, the success of the restaurant will depend on ______.

SUMMARIZING

Summarizing is a good way to check your comprehension. When you write a summary, you include only the main information and not the details. A summary is shorter than the original reading.

Imagine this: You and a friend go to Laura's restaurant for lunch. You can see Laura, wearing dark sunglasses, cooking your food. You know Laura's story; your friend does not. While you are eating, you tell your friend what you know about Laura. Complete the summary below on a separate piece of paper. Include only the main information and not the details.

The chef's name is Laura Martinez. She is blind because she had cancer in both eyes when she was a baby. She was born in Mexico but came to the United States when she was a girl. . . .

NEWS AND VIEWS

In this unit, you have read about Chef Laura Martinez, who realized that food was her passion.

Laura's story would not surprise Parker Palmer. Dr. Palmer is a teacher and writer who believes he knows how people can find work that will bring them joy. According to Dr. Palmer, the way to find work that is right for you is to become "the person you have always been."

Before you read, think about what Dr. Palmer means by becoming "the person you have always been."

Becoming Yourself

1 Every time Parker Palmer's little granddaughter comes to visit, he observes her. He notices what she likes and doesn't like. He notices how she moves, what she does, and what she says. Then he writes his observations down. When his granddaughter is older, he will put his observations in a letter and give the letter to her. His letter will begin something like this: "Here is a sketch of who you were from your earliest days in the world. It is not a complete picture—only you can draw that. But it was sketched by a person who loves you very much. Perhaps these notes will help you do what I finally did in my own life: Remember who you were when you first arrived and reclaim the gift of true self."

2 Dr. Palmer will give his granddaughter the letter when she is in her late teens or early 20s, when she will probably be deciding what kind of work she wants to do. Dr. Palmer hopes that if his granddaughter knows her "true self," she will choose work that is right for her.

continued ▶

A future astronomer?

3 Young people who are trying to decide on a career often ask themselves, "What should I do with my life?" Dr. Palmer thinks it is more useful to ask, "Who am I? What is my nature?" He points out that everything in the universe has a nature, which has its limits as well as its potentials. This is a truth that people who work daily with natural materials know. A potter, for example, cannot simply tell the clay what to do. The clay presses back on the potter's hands, telling her what it can and cannot do. If she fails to listen to the clay, her pottery will be frail and unattractive. An engineer cannot tell his materials what they must do. He must understand the nature of the steel or the wood or the stone he is working with. If he does not, the bridge or building he designs could collapse. Human beings, Dr. Palmer says, also have a nature, with limits as well as potentials. When choosing a career, we must understand the material we are working with, just as the potter understands the clay and the engineer the steel. To find work that is right for us, we must know our nature. Attempts to override that nature always fail.

4 It is not always easy for us to know exactly what our nature is. Sometimes we are discouraged from following our natural inclinations, and we lose track of what they are. When we are young, we are surrounded by expectations—the expectations of our families, our teachers, and, later, our employers. Often these people are not trying to understand our nature; instead, they are trying to fit us into slots. Sometimes racism, sexism, or tradition determines the slots people choose for us. For example, a little girl who wants to be a carpenter when she grows up is told that girls cannot be carpenters, but she could be a teacher. Or an oldest son who wants to be an artist is persuaded to take over the family business instead of studying art. We feel the pressure of others' expectations, and we betray our nature in order to be accepted.

5 Dr. Palmer maintains that if we lose track of our true self, it is possible to pick up the trail again. One way is to look for clues from our younger years, when we lived closer to our nature. That is how he found his way back to his true self. In his book *Let Your Life Speak*, he writes:

6 In grade school, I became fascinated with the mysteries of flight. As many boys did in those days, I spent endless hours, after school and on weekends, designing, making, flying, and (usually) crashing model airplanes made of fragile wood.

7 Unlike most boys, however, I also spent long hours creating eight- and twelve-page books about aviation. I would turn a sheet of paper sideways; draw a vertical line down the middle; make diagrams of, say, the cross-section of a wing; roll the sheet into a typewriter; and type a caption explaining how air moving across the wing creates a vacuum that lifts the plane. Then I would fold that sheet in half along with several others I had made, staple the collection together down the spine, and painstakingly illustrate the cover.

8 I had always thought that the meaning of this paperwork was obvious: fascinated with flight, I wanted to be a pilot, or perhaps an aeronautical engineer. But recently, when I found a couple of these books in a cardboard box, I suddenly saw the truth, and it was more obvious than I had imagined. I didn't want to be a pilot or anything related to aviation. I wanted to be an author, to make books—a task I have been attempting from the third grade to this very moment!

9 When he found the books he had made as a boy, Parker Palmer realized that for most of his adult life he had not been following his natural inclinations. He says that he tried to ignore his nature, hide from it, and run from it, and he thinks he is not alone. He believes that there is a universal tendency to want to be someone else—but that it is more important to be oneself.

10 And so, Dr. Palmer observes his granddaughter. He hopes that someday his observations will help her remember what she was like when she was very young. He hopes that she will become the person she was born to be and find work that will bring her joy. He hopes, in short, that she will grow up to be the person she has always been.

BUILDING VOCABULARY

IDENTIFYING THE CORRECT DEFINITION

Read each sentence. What is the meaning of the boldfaced word? Choose from several meanings this word can have.* Circle the letter of the correct answer.

1. It is not always easy for us to know exactly what our **nature** is.
   a. everything in the physical world that is not controlled by humans, such as wild plants and animals, earth and rocks, and the weather: *I've always been a nature lover.*
   b. the qualities that make someone different from others: *It's her nature to be generous.*

2. Parker Palmer's letter to his granddaughter will begin, "Here is a **sketch** of who you were from your earliest days in the world."
   a. a simple, quickly made drawing that does not show much detail: *These are Renoir's sketches for his paintings.*
   b. a short written or spoken description: *The speaker gave us a sketch of life in the 1890s.*

3. We feel the **pressure** of others' expectations.
   a. an attempt to persuade someone by using influence, arguments, or threats: *So far, she has resisted pressure to tell her story to the newspapers.*
   b. the force or weight that is being put on something: *To stop the bleeding, put pressure directly on the wound.*
   c. the weight of the air: *Low pressure often brings rain.*

4. We **betray** our nature in order to be accepted.
   a. to be disloyal to someone who trusts you, so that they are hurt or upset: *She betrayed her friend when she told everyone his secret.*
   b. to be disloyal to your country, for example by giving secret information to its enemies: *He betrayed his country for money.*
   c. to stop supporting your beliefs and principles, especially in order to get power or avoid trouble: *He said he would always tell the truth, but he betrayed his principles when he lied to me.*
   d. to show feelings that you are trying to hide: *His face betrayed his disappointment at not getting the job.*

5. Dr. Palmer **maintains** that if we lose track of our true self, it is possible to pick up the trail again.
   a. to make something continue in the same way as before: *They hope to maintain peace in the region.*
   b. to take care of something so that it stays in good condition: *They maintain all the equipment in the office.*
   c. to strongly express your belief that something is true: *For centuries people maintained that the world was flat.*

* The definitions are adapted from the *Longman Advanced American Dictionary*.

6. "I would staple the collection of papers together down the **spine**."
   a. the row of bones down the center of the back of humans and some animals: *The human spine is made up of 33 separate bones.*
   b. the side of a book where the pages are fastened together: *What you see on a library shelf is a book's spine.*
   c. a stiff, sharp-pointed part of an animal or plant: *Touching a cactus spine can be a painful experience!*

DEVELOPING READING SKILLS

UNDERSTANDING THE MAIN IDEAS

There is one correct way to complete each sentence or answer each question. Circle the letter of the correct answer.

1. Parker Palmer believes that to find work that is right for us, we must
   a. know our nature.
   b. meet our families' expectations.
   c. work with natural materials.
2. According to Dr. Palmer, it is sometimes difficult for us to know our nature because
   a. our parents and grandparents do not take the time to observe us and tell us what our nature is.
   b. our families, teachers, and employers discourage us from following our natural inclinations, and we no longer remember what our nature is.
   c. human beings, unlike natural materials, do not always have a nature.
3. Imagine that a 21-year-old man tells Dr. Palmer that he doesn't know exactly what his nature is. What would Dr. Palmer tell him to do?
   a. "Ask your family and teachers, 'What should I do with my life?'"
   b. "Don't try to discover your nature; attempts to discover it always fail."
   c. "Look for clues in your childhood; try to remember what you liked and didn't like when you were young."
4. When Parker Palmer found his old books in a cardboard box, he realized that
   a. he should have become a pilot or an aeronautical engineer.
   b. he did not use his free time wisely when he was a boy.
   c. he had not followed his natural inclinations for most of his adult life.
5. Why is Parker Palmer observing his granddaughter and writing down his observations?
   a. He is a writer, and he will include his observations in a book about finding the right work.
   b. He believes his observations will help her choose the right work when she is older.
   c. He believes that he might not be alive when she is an adult and wants her to remember their time together.

EVALUATING STATEMENTS

A The following statements reflect Parker Palmer's opinions. Read each statement and check (✓) *Agree* or *Disagree*.

	Agree	Disagree
1. To find work that is right for us, we must know our nature.	☐	☐
2. It is not always easy for us to know what our nature is.	☐	☐
3. We sometimes feel the pressure of others' expectations, and we betray our nature in order to be accepted.	☐	☐
4. If we lose track of our "true self," one way to pick up the trail is to look for clues in our younger years.	☐	☐

B Compare your answers with a partner's. Explain to your partner why you agree or disagree. If you have had an experience that supports your opinion, tell your partner about it.

APPLYING INFORMATION

The boy in the photo loves to help his father work on the family car. He's been helping his father fix cars and trucks ever since he could walk.

Discuss the answers to these questions with your classmates, or write your answers on a separate piece of paper.

1. Would Parker Palmer say that the boy should be a mechanic when he grows up?
2. Do you think the boy should be a mechanic when he grows up?

READING A CHART

The jobs in the list below are among the 100 best jobs in the United States.* Why are they considered the best? The jobs were rated in five categories. In each category, the jobs were scored 1 to 10, with 10 being the best score. The jobs with the highest overall scores made the "best jobs" list.

A **Read the descriptions of the categories.**

1. **Salary:** A high score means workers in this field make the most money.
2. **Job market:** A high score means it's easier to find a job in this field.
3. **Future growth:** A high score means it will probably be easier to find a job in this field in the future.
4. **Stress level:** A high score means *low* stress.
5. **Work-life balance:** A high score means workers in this field have free time for family, friends, and leisure.

B **Read the chart.**

Job	Salary	Job Market	Future Growth	Stress Level	Work-Life Balance
Doctor	10.0	4	6	2	6
Interpreter / Translator[1]	5.4	6	6	6	10
Medical Assistant[2]	4.4	10	8	6	6
Personal Care Aide[3]	3.7	10	10	4	6
Plumber	5.7	8	6	6	8
Software Developer[4]	7.9	10	10	6	8
Web Developer[5]	6.4	6	6	8	10
Wind Turbine Technician[6]	5.7	4	10	8	6

1 An interpreter works in spoken language; a translator works in written language.

2 A medical assistant does office work—for example, answering the phone—and may also do some medical procedures—for example, drawing blood.

3 A personal care aide helps elderly people or people with chronic diseases with everyday tasks—for example, getting dressed.

4 A software developer invents technologies—for example, apps for smart phones.

5 A web developer creates websites.

6 A wind turbine technician inspects, maintains, and repairs wind turbines.

* According to *U.S. News & World Report.*

C **Answer the questions below.**

1. Which is the highest-paying job? doctor
2. Which is the lowest-paying job? ______
3. Which two jobs are the least stressful? ______
4. Which two jobs give people the best work-life balance? ______
5. Which three jobs are the easiest to find now? ______
6. Which three jobs will be the easiest to find in the future? ______

D **Discuss the answers to these questions with your classmates.**

1. These “best jobs” are in the United States. Are there any jobs on the list that would not be the best jobs in your native country? Cross them out. Then compare your list with that of a classmate from another country.
2. Are the high-paying jobs in the United States also high-paying jobs in your native country?
3. What do you think about the five categories (salary, job market, future growth, stress, work-life balance) that were used to rate the jobs? Which category is most important to you? Are there other categories that should have been considered, too?
4. If you discovered that the work you want to do is not on a list like the one above, would you consider choosing different work? Why or why not?
5. What do you think Parker Palmer would think of this list?

DISCUSSION

Parker Palmer believes that you must know your nature if you want to find work that is right for you. One way to discover what he calls your “true self” is to look for clues in your younger years. He gives himself as an example: He was a boy who made books in his free time; that was a clue that he should be an author.

A **Find five ways to complete the sentence, “I was a kid who…” Write your answers on the lines.**

Example:

I was a kid who

1. was very shy.
2. was neat and tidy.
3. was diligent.
4. hated sports.
5. liked taking things apart to see how they worked.

I was a kid who

1. ______________________________

2. ______________________________

3. ______________________________

4. ______________________________

5. ______________________________

B Read your description of yourself as a child to a small group of classmates. Then tell your classmates what kind of work you want to do (or already do). Do you and your classmates see clues in your description that you have chosen work that is right for you? What are the clues?

WRITING

Choose one of the following topics to write about.

1. What kind of work do you plan to do? (Or, what kind of work do you do?) Explain why you chose that work.
2. Laura Martinez worked hard to achieve her goal of being a chef. Imagine this: It is ten years from now. You have worked hard, and you are successful in your career. Where are you, and what are you doing? What did you do to get to where you are? Write about your future life.
3. In an interview, Laura Martinez said that when she was a little girl, she would run into the kitchen to help whenever she heard her grandmother, aunts, and mother cooking. Can you look back on a childhood experience and see that the right work for you was already clear then? Describe your experience.
4. Ask someone who knew you when you were a child to describe what you were like when you were very young. Ask the person to describe anything special that you said or did. Write their memories of you.
5. Can you think of people in your own life who have found work they love? Describe one of those people and the work he or she does.
6. Interview someone about his or her work. First, make a list of possible questions you could ask, for example:
   - What do you do on a typical workday?
   - What do you like about your work?
   - What don't you like about your work?
   - Why did you choose this work?

   Record your interview or take notes. At home, listen to the recording or review your notes. Then decide what information you would like to include in a short essay about the person you interviewed. (You might want to focus on the answer to only one of your questions.)

UNIT 3

Geeks

The theme of this unit is geeks. The word *geek* has had different meanings over time. In the past, a geek was someone who behaved awkwardly and had strange interests. Today, a geek is someone who is passionate about technology and has a talent for working with computers.

Discuss the answers to these questions with your classmates. If you don't understand the meaning of the words in boldface, work individually, in a small group, or as a class to find out what they mean.

1. Do you use **e-mail**? If so, how many e-mails do you get every day? Who sends you e-mail?
2. Do you send **text messages**? If so, how many do you send every day?
3. Do you follow any **blogs**? If so, what topics are the blogs about?
4. Do you sometimes take **selfies**? If so, where did you take your favorite selfie?
5. Have you ever **googled** your own name? If so, did any results surprise you?
6. Are appliances in your house (your TV, for example) connected to the **Internet**? If so, which appliances are connected?
7. Do you have a **smartphone**? If so, where is it while you sleep? How soon after you wake up do you check it?

Technology is now a part of many people's lives all over the world. In this unit, you will learn about the people who invent, improve, and maintain that technology. First, you will read the story of two young men whose talent for working with computers brought them phenomenal success. Then you will learn what geeks are and what they are not. (Perhaps you will discover that you or someone you know is a geek!)

A TRUE STORY IN THE NEWS

David Filo and Jerry Yang

PRE-READING

The young men in the photo had a talent for working with computers, and that talent brought them phenomenal success.

A **Look at the photo and read the title of the story on the next page. With your classmates, make a list of questions you think the story will answer.**

Example:

1. *Who are David Filo and Jerry Yang?*
2. *How long ago was the photo taken?*

B **When you have finished reading the story, look back at the questions you and your classmates wrote. Which questions did the story answer?**

Two Yahoos

1 Imagine a Hollywood movie with this plot: Lily Yang, a young widow, leaves Taiwan and immigrates to the United States, hoping her son, Chih-Yuan, will have a better life there. After the family settles in California, Chih-Yuan changes his first name to Jerry and heads off to school, knowing only one word of English, the word *shoe*. Jerry learns English quickly; he is exceptionally bright and becomes a straight-A student. When he graduates from high school, he wins a scholarship to a top university, where he becomes friends with David Filo, a fellow student. Together Jerry and David start an Internet company that makes them both billionaires within five years.

2 If you think this could happen only in a Hollywood movie, you are wrong. It could happen in California's Silicon Valley.[1] And it did.

3 In 1993, Jerry Yang and David Filo were studying for their doctorates in electrical engineering at Stanford University in California. They did their work side by side at desks that the university provided for them. But when they sat down at their computers, they often found themselves "surfing the Web"—looking for interesting sites on the Internet, which was new then—instead of working, like two kids watching TV rather than doing their homework.

4 Jerry and David thought the Internet was fascinating and at the same time frustrating. They were constantly asking each other, "Hey—where was that cool page we saw the other day?" Sometimes it would take them hours to find a Web site again. The problem was this: The only way to get to an Internet site was to type in its exact address (called its *URL*, for "universal resource locator"). A URL could be a long string of numbers and letters like this: *http://www.wnn.or.jp/wnn-t/index_e.html*. If the address was not perfectly right—if one letter was left out or one dot was misplaced—it was impossible to get to that Web site. Imagine a library with no system for organizing books. The only way to find a book would be to know exactly where it was. That was the state of the Internet in 1993.

5 David developed software so that Jerry could compile a list of their favorite Web sites; that way, they could revisit them whenever they wanted to. Jerry kept adding sites to the list, and it quickly got so long that it needed to be organized. Jerry thought back to a part-time job he'd had shelving books in the university library. He remembered how the books were organized into categories and subcategories, and he decided to organize his list of Web sites in the same way. "Sports," for example, became one category, with subcategories like "sumo wrestling" and "basketball."

6 Jerry called the list "Jerry's Guide to the World Wide Web" and posted it on the Internet in the spring of 1994. Friends told friends about "Jerry's Guide," and the number of people viewing it doubled every month—from hundreds, to thousands, to hundreds of thousands. Telephone calls and e-mails suggesting sites to add were coming in faster than Jerry and David could handle them. Jerry and David abandoned their studies altogether and started working 20 hours a day on Jerry's list, often sleeping on the floor next to their computers. Their hobby had become an obsession.

7 Late one night, Jerry and David began talking about changing the name of the Web site. "Jerry's Guide to the World Wide Web" no longer seemed appropriate, as David was working on the site as much as Jerry. They flipped through a dictionary, looking for possible new names, and came across the word *yahoo*. The dictionary gave two definitions of the word: "a rough or noisy person" and "a word shouted when you find something you're excited about." They liked the word—they thought it reflected the Wild West nature of the Internet. Just for fun, they added an exclamation point. Yahoo!, they

continued ▶

1 *Silicon Valley* = an area of California between San Francisco and San Jose that is a center of the computer industry.

thought, was a name people would remember. Indeed it was.

8 By the end of 1994, the Yahoo! Web site was getting one million hits a day, and Stanford's computer system was crashing under the strain. University officials told Jerry and David they would have to move their hobby off campus. When word got out that Yahoo! was looking for a new home, Jerry and David got job offers from several giant telecommunications companies. The offer they finally accepted, however, was not a job offer, but an offer of money. A venture capitalist gave Jerry and David $1 million to start their own business. In exchange, he took a 25 percent stake in Yahoo! Yahoo!, the corporation, was born.

9 When Yahoo! officially opened for business, its corporate offices were typical for an Internet start-up company. Newspaper accounts from 1995 give this description:

> All the office furniture is purple and yellow, the official corporate colors. In purple-painted cubicles, 16 employees, called "surfers," sit in front of computers and review Web site submissions, rejecting some and deciding where to put the ones they accept. All of the surfers are in their early 20s, wear T-shirts, and park their bicycles next to their desks. From time to time, David Filo, barefoot and wearing torn jeans, emerges from his office, which is cluttered with old newspapers, a pair of purple roller blades, and crumpled Coke cans. It is decorated with a replica of a large fish. Often David doesn't leave Yahoo! headquarters for days—he sleeps under his desk—and when he does leave, he drives away in a dilapidated old car, its tailpipe dragging on the ground. Jerry wears jeans and a green plastic Yahoo! watch. To top it off, Jerry and David carry business cards that identify their positions in the company as the "Chief Yahoos."

10 But the Chief Yahoos knew what they were doing. Their competitors were in a race to develop powerful technology to collect as many Internet sites as possible for their directories. Some even used robot computers, called "spiders," that searched the Internet day and night, looking for new sites. Yahoo! thought its competitors were on the wrong track. Jerry and David suspected that people didn't necessarily want access to every site on the Internet; they needed help sorting through all the sites that were out there. That is what Yahoo! would do. Instead of buying robot computers, Yahoo! hired more people. People, not software programs, would choose Web sites for the Yahoo! directory and put them in the appropriate categories. The final work would always be done by humans.

11 Jerry and David's instincts were right. Yahoo! became the most popular site on the World Wide Web, attracting 100 million people a month. These were the huge numbers advertisers wanted, and corporations started paying millions for advertising spots on the Yahoo! site. Yahoo! was a gold mine, and Jerry and David had struck it rich.

12 During the next decades, Yahoo!'s fortunes went up and down. Yahoo! struggled to compete with Google, which ultimately became a more popular search engine than Yahoo! In 2017, Yahoo! was sold and the company was renamed. Still, the story of Yahoo! will always be an important part of Internet history. We have Jerry Yang and David Filo to thank for making Internet searches easier and search results better organized.

13 So the next time you're searching the Internet and find exactly what you're looking for in seconds, you might want to think about Jerry and David. And, in honor of them, you just might want to shout, "Yahoo!"

GETTING THE BIG PICTURE

What are the reasons for Jerry and David's phenomenal success with Yahoo!? Check (✓) three reasons.

☐ 1. Jerry and David were bright and had a talent for working with computers.

☐ 2. They had doctorates in computer science and years of experience working with computers.

☐ 3. They worked hard—sometimes 20 hours a day.

☐ 4. They got help from giant telecommunications companies.

☐ 5. They were among the first to develop a way to organize sites on the Internet and help people find Web sites.

BUILDING VOCABULARY

RECALLING NEW WORDS

Read each sentence. What is the meaning of the word(s) in *italics*? Write the letter of your answer on the line.

__f__ 1. After they entered the United States, the Yang family decided to *settle* in California.

____ 2. David Filo was *a fellow* student at Stanford University.

____ 3. In 1993, the only way to find an Internet site was to know its exact address. That was the *state* of the Internet then.

____ 4. Jerry and David were *flipping through* the dictionary, searching for a name for their Web site.

____ 5. Jerry and David got $1 million from a *venture capitalist.*

____ 6. The man gave Jerry and David $1 million, and they gave him a 25 percent *stake in* Yahoo!.

____ 7. Yahoo!'s employees worked in *cubicles.*

____ 8. Often David didn't leave Yahoo!'s *headquarters* for days.

____ 9. David's office was decorated with a *replica* of a large fish.

____ 10. Jerry and David thought their competitors were *on the wrong track.*

____ 11. Yahoo! had become a *gold mine*, and Jerry and David had struck it rich.

a. small, partly enclosed spaces in a large office

b. person who lends money to people who want to start their own business

c. business that produces large profits

d. also a

e. exact copy

f. make their home

g. share of

h. condition

i. doing things that made it unlikely they would succeed

j. quickly turning the pages of

k. main office

UNDERSTANDING SPECIAL EXPRESSIONS

Complete the sentences to show that you understand the meanings of the new words. There may be several correct ways to complete each sentence.

1. ***to come across*** **= to discover by chance**

   Example: While looking through a pile of books that were on sale, I came across one that I'd been wanting to read for a long time.

   a. Jerry and David were flipping through a dictionary, looking for a new name for their Web site, when they came across ______________________________.

   b. While looking through an old photo album, he came across ______________________________.

   c. While cleaning my closet, I came across ______________________________.

2. ***word got out*** **= many people heard**

   Example: When word got out that the new nuclear power plant would be only one mile from the town, environmental groups protested.

   a. When word got out that Yahoo! was looking for a new home, Jerry and David ______________________________.

   b. When word got out that the new store would give free TVs to its first 100 customers, ______________________________.

   c. When word got out that the professor had given a failing grade to everyone in the class, ______________________________.

3. ***to top it off*** **= in addition to all the other unusual things that happened**

   Example: When I took a shower, there was no hot water. To top it off, the shampoo bottle was empty.

   a. At first, Yahoo! didn't seem like a serious company: The office was purple and yellow, the employees wore T-shirts, and David Filo walked around barefoot. To top it off, ______________________________.

   b. On the day of the picnic, it rained and the weather turned cold. To top it off, ______________________________.

   c. On the day of the exam, I overslept and then missed the bus. To top it off, ______________________________.

DEVELOPING READING SKILLS

UNDERSTANDING THE MAIN IDEAS

The story of Yahoo! is an important part of Internet history. Reporters sometimes interview Jerry Yang to ask him about the early days of the company.

Imagine this: You are Jerry Yang, and a reporter asks you the questions below. Write your answers to the reporter's questions on a separate piece of paper. The first one is done for you.

1. You once said that you and David found the Internet "frustrating" in its early days. Why was it frustrating?

   To get to an Internet site, you had to know its exact address. Sometimes David and I would find a really cool Web page, and then a few days later we couldn't find it again.

2. I understand that Yahoo! began as a list of Web sites that you organized. How did you organize them?
3. When Yahoo! opened for business in 1995, its corporate offices were described as "typical for an Internet start-up." What did the offices look like?
4. How was Yahoo! different from its competitors?

SCANNING FOR INFORMATION

Scanning is reading quickly to find specific information. If, for example, you wanted the answer to the question, "Which university did Jerry and David attend?" you could scan the story for the information. You would move your eyes quickly across the pages, perhaps looking for words that begin with a capital letter, until you found "Stanford"—the information you wanted.

Scan the story for the words below. Think of questions that would give you these answers. Write your questions on the lines.

Question	Answer
1. *What is Jerry's Chinese name?*	Chih-Yuan
2. ______	"sumo wrestling" and "basketball"
3. ______	in the spring of 1994
4. ______	"a rough or noisy person"
5. ______	purple and yellow
6. ______	"Chief Yahoos"
7. ______	"spiders"
8. ______	Google
9. ______	in 2017

MAKING INFERENCES

To *infer* is to use information you have to make a logical guess. For example, let's say Jerry Yang is being interviewed on TV. He says, "When we came here, she didn't know how she would earn a living. She was very brave." You know from the story that Jerry and his mother came from Taiwan, so you can infer that he is talking about his mother. You cannot be sure he is talking about her, but it would be a logical guess.

Jerry Yang made the following statements to reporters in interviews. (The statements are not in the story.) Use the information you know from the story to infer what he is talking about. Write your answers on the lines.

1. "**It** started because David got sick of me asking him where everything was."

   What is "it"? "Jerry's Guide to the World Wide Web," which later became Yahoo!

2. "A lot of people found **it** easy to remember, which we thought was probably good."

   What is "it"? ______________________________

3. "**This place** has an energy that I don't want to lose; it's full of young people who want to change the world as much as I do. That's what I love."

   What is "this place"? ______________________________

4. "We've been through some tough times, but we've never had rough times together. There was hardly ever any tension between **him** and me. It's just a fantastic relationship, and I hope it's a lifelong one."

   Who is "him"? ______________________________

RESPONDING TO THE READING

A **Answer the questions by checking (✓) *Yes* or *No*.**

	Yes	No
1. When they were only six months from finishing their doctorates in electrical engineering, Jerry and David abandoned their studies to work on "Jerry's Guide to the World Wide Web." If you were only six months from finishing a university degree, would you quit your studies to do something you were more interested in?	☐	☐
2. Jerry and David worked 20 hours a day on Jerry's list. Would you sit at a computer for hours and hours if you were working on something you were really interested in?	☐	☐
3. Jerry and David didn't accept high-paying jobs with large corporations; instead, they started their own company. If you were offered a high-paying job with a large corporation, would you say, "No, thank you," and start your own company instead?	☐	☐
4. Even after Jerry and David had their own company, David still drove a dilapidated old car, and Jerry wore a green plastic watch. If you suddenly became wealthy, would you still drive an old car and wear a cheap plastic watch?	☐	☐

B **Compare your answers with a partner's. Explain why you checked *Yes* or *No*. Then count how many times you checked *Yes*. Who is more like Jerry and David, you or your partner?**

NEWS AND VIEWS

You have read about Jerry Yang and David Filo, who know a lot about technology and computers. Do you think they probably have some personality traits in common? Do computers and technology attract a certain type of person? Are you one of those people?

Is technology your passion? Are you the one friends call when their computer screens freeze up, or when they have lost an important computer file? Do you want to be a computer programmer or Web site designer, or are you already one? Do you work, or want to work, in the technical support department of a corporation, hospital, or university? If you answered "yes" to any of these questions, you might be a geek.

In his book *Geeks*, technology writer Jon Katz describes what a geek is.

As you read, think about this: Does Jon Katz's description of a geek fit you or someone you know?

From *Geeks* by Jon Katz

What is a geek?

1 In the early 1900s, geeks were destitute, homeless men who worked at circuses and carnivals. They bit the heads off chickens and rats in exchange for food or a place to sleep. Later the word *geek* was used to describe anyone who was strange or nonconformist. Then, sometime in the 1990s, the meaning of the word changed again: Today, a geek is someone who is passionate about technology and has a talent for working with computers.

2 I have met and corresponded with thousands of geeks, and I still can't answer the question, "What exactly is a geek?" I can only make some general observations on what today's geeks are, and what they are not.

3 For one thing, geeks are not the asocial loners some people think they are. You can hardly be a geek all by yourself. The online world is one giant community comprised of hundreds of thousands of smaller ones, all involving connections to other people. The geekiest hangouts on the Internet are hive-like communities of worker geeks patching together cheap and efficient new software that they share freely and generously with one another. That's not something loners could or would do.

4 Geeks are smart. I've met skinny and fat geeks, shy and outgoing ones, cheerful and grumpy ones—but never dumb ones.

5 Geeks are not like other people. They've grown up in the freest media environment ever. They talk openly about politics and criticize revered leaders. They defy government, business, or any other institution to shut down their freewheeling culture.

Are you a geek?

6 People e-mail me all the time asking if they are geeks.

7 I figure people have the right to name themselves; if you feel like a geek, you are one. But here are some clues: You are online a good part of the time. You feel a personal connection with technology, not with the machines themselves, but with what the machines can do. You like to watch *The Simpsons* on TV and you like the *Star Wars* movies. You are obsessive about pop culture, which is what you talk about with your friends or coworkers every Monday.

8 You don't like being told what to do because you believe that people in authority are

continued ▶

generally not on your side. Life began for you when you got out of high school, which, more likely than not, was a painful experience. You didn't go to dances, or if you did, you certainly didn't feel comfortable there. Maybe your parents helped you get through, maybe a teacher or a soul mate.

9 Now, you zone out on your work. You solve problems and puzzles. You love to create things just for the kick of it. Even though you're indispensable to the company that's hired you, it's almost impossible to imagine yourself running it. You may have power of your own now—a family, money—yet you see yourself as an outsider, one who never quite fits in. In many ways, geekdom is a state of mind—a sense of yourself in relation to the world.

What does the future hold for geeks?

10 More and more, the world depends on computers and the people who run them. As a result, geeks have almost limitless job prospects. The U.S. Department of Labor predicts that over the next several years the fastest-growing occupations will be in the computer field.

11 Geeks are literally building the new global economy, constructing and expanding the Internet and the World Wide Web as well as maintaining it. They're paid well for their skills: Starting salaries for college grads with computer degrees are high, and the demand is so great that many geeks forgo or abandon college. Elite universities like Caltech, Stanford, and MIT complain that some of their best students abandon graduate school for high-paying positions in technology industries.

12 Until now, geeks were thought to be unglamorous and have never had great status or influence. But the Internet is the hottest and hippest place in American culture, and the people who were formerly outsiders are now insiders. Geeks are often the only ones able to operate our most complex and vital computer systems, and their work will be in demand for years to come.

13 For the first time ever, it's a great time to be a geek.

BUILDING VOCABULARY

UNDERSTANDING ACADEMIC VOCABULARY

The words below are on the Academic Word List. Find the words in "Geeks." (The number in parentheses is the number of the paragraph.) If you are not sure what a word means, look it up in your dictionary. Then use the words in the sentences that follow.

comprises (3)	predict (10)	expanded (11)	abandon (11)
environment (5)	global (11)	maintain (11)	status (12)
authority (8)	construct (11)		

1. When his car broke down, he had to ___abandon___ it at the side of the road and walk all the way home.
2. Temperatures are rising all over the world, and many scientists are concerned about ____________ warming.
3. The city's school system, which ____________ two high schools, three middle schools, and four elementary schools, is considered one of the best in the state.
4. She has a lot of power in her position in the company, but she cannot fire workers who are not doing their jobs well; only the president of the company has the ____________ to do that.
5. The company has redecorated its offices and installed brighter lighting so that its employees will have a more pleasant ____________ in which to work.
6. The highway goes right through the center of the town, but there are plans to ____________ a new highway that will go around the town.
7. Some people drive a luxury car so that others know how rich or how important they are. The car is a ____________ symbol.
8. The old engine had a lot of moving parts, so it was not easy to take care of. The new engine has fewer moving parts and should be easier to ____________.
9. The company used to sell its chocolate only in Switzerland. But over the years, the business ____________, and now the chocolate is sold all over Europe.
10. Before a storm, animals often become restless and will not lie down. Some farmers say they can ____________ the weather by watching their animals.

UNDERSTANDING SLANG EXPRESSIONS

Find these slang expressions in the article. (The number in parentheses is the number of the paragraph.) Then read the expressions in the new contexts below. Finally, complete the definition of each slang expression. The first one is done for you.

a loner (3) hangout (3) zone out (9) just for the kick of it (9)

1. He's a loner. We've invited him to parties, but he never comes. He seems happiest when he's by himself, watching a movie or working at his computer.

   A "loner" is a person who prefers to be alone ______.

2. The swimming pool is a popular hangout. In the summer, a lot of teenagers spend their afternoons there, swimming, talking, and eating snacks.

   A "hangout" is a place where people ______

   ______.

3. I completely zoned out on my work. I forgot to eat lunch and didn't even notice that it had gotten late and the room was getting dark.

   If you "zone out" on your work, you ______

   ______.

4. Just for the kick of it, we decided to run to the bus stop, even though we had plenty of time to walk.

   If you do something "just for the kick of it," you do it ______

   ______.

DEVELOPING READING SKILLS

UNDERSTANDING THE MAIN IDEAS

There are three correct ways to complete each sentence. Cross out the one incorrect answer.

1. Jon Katz
   a. writes about technology and is the author of a book titled *Geeks*.
   b. ~~knows exactly what a geek is because he is one.~~
   c. has met and corresponded with thousands of geeks.
   d. says he can't answer the question, "What exactly is a geek?"
2. Some definitions of the word *geek* are
   a. poor, homeless men who worked at circuses and carnivals in exchange for food or a place to sleep.
   b. anyone who is strange or nonconformist.
   c. anyone who has extreme political opinions.
   d. someone who is passionate about technology and has a talent for working with computers.

3. When people ask Jon Katz if they are geeks, he
   a. tells them, "You are a geek if you feel like one."
   b. gives them clues that tell them if they are geeks.
   c. tells them what geeks typically do.
   d. tells them that the word *geek* is impossible to define.

4. Today is a great time to be a geek because they
   a. easily get into top universities, like Caltech and MIT.
   b. have almost limitless job prospects.
   c. are paid well for their skills.
   d. are constructing and expanding the Internet, the hottest place in American culture.

UNDERSTANDING DETAILS

The people in the photo say they are geeks. According to the author of *Geeks*, what are they like, and what do they typically do? On a separate piece of paper, write at least eight sentences that describe these people.

Examples:

They are smart.
They are online a lot.

READING A BAR GRAPH

Slashdot is a Web site for people who are interested in technology. (Most of them describe themselves as geeks.) Often there is a question at the Slashdot Web site. Visitors to the site answer the question, and the next day Slashdot reports their answers. Usually between 10,000 to 30,000 people answer the question.

Here are some questions Slashdot asked on its Web site. Read the questions and graphs. Then write a sentence about each graph that tells how the largest number of people who come to the Slashdot Web site answered each question. The first one is done for you.

1. **How old are you?**

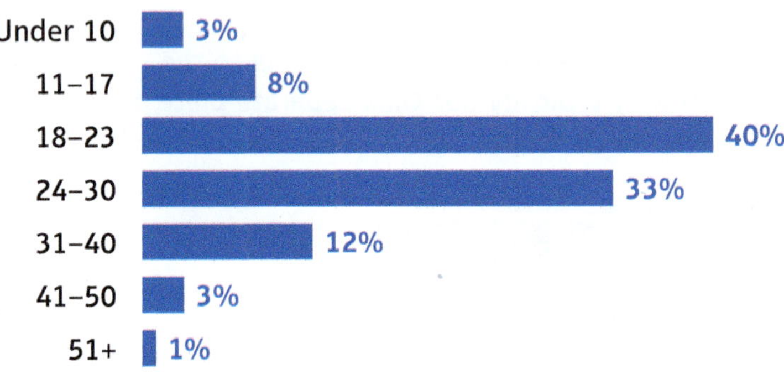

The largest number of people are between 18 and 23 years old.

2. **How soon after you wake up do you check your phone?**

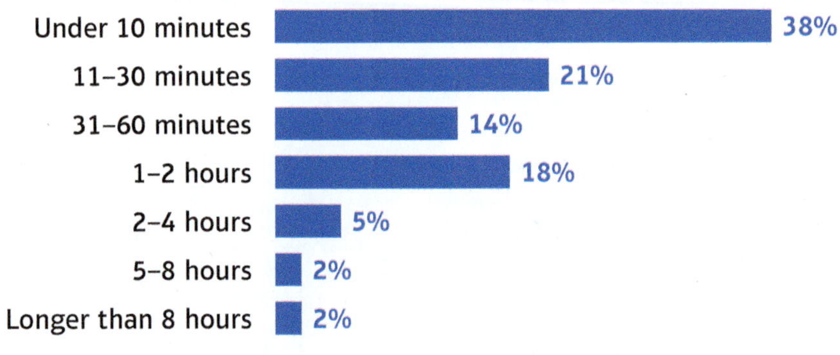

____

3. **How long is your usual workday?**

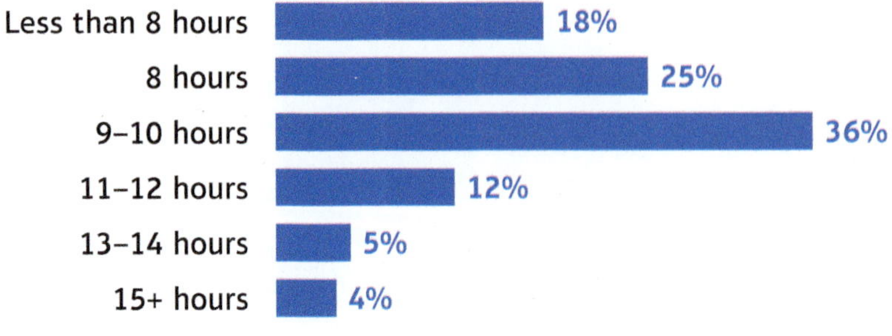

____

4. **What do you wear to work?**

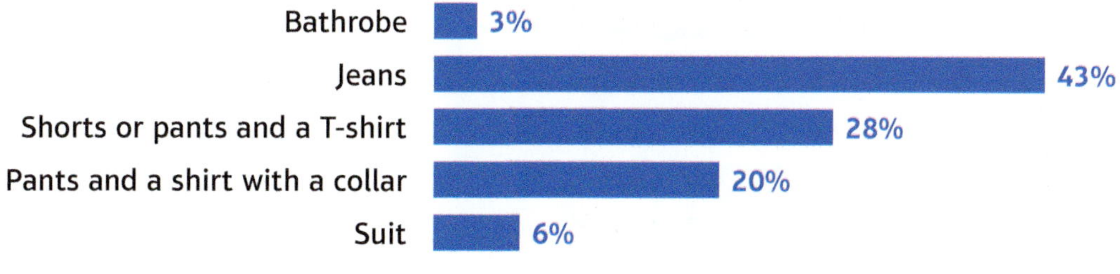

5. **I sit in front of a screen for ______ of my waking time.**

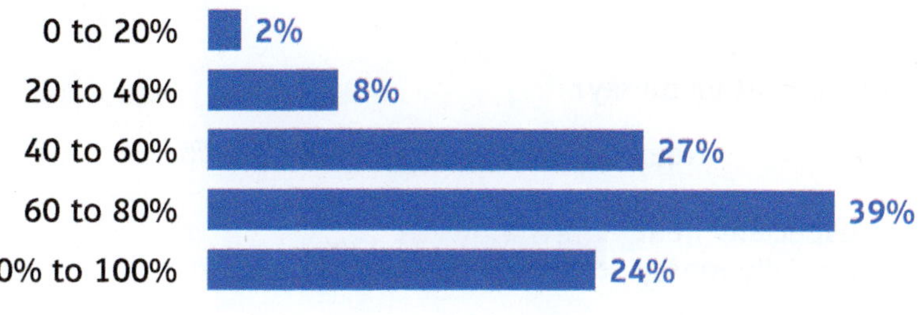

6. **How often do friends and family call you for tech support?**

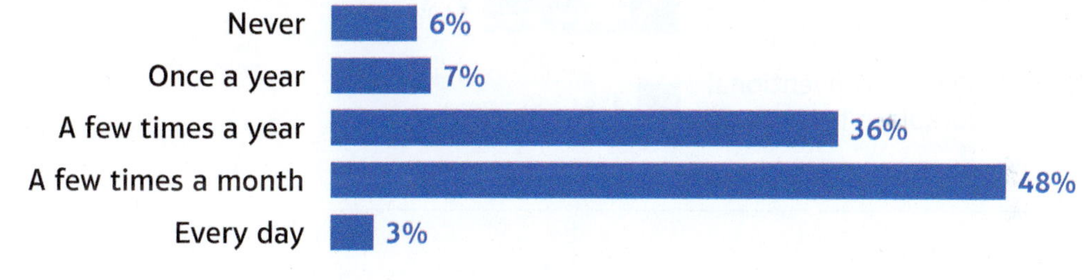

7. **How smart are you?**

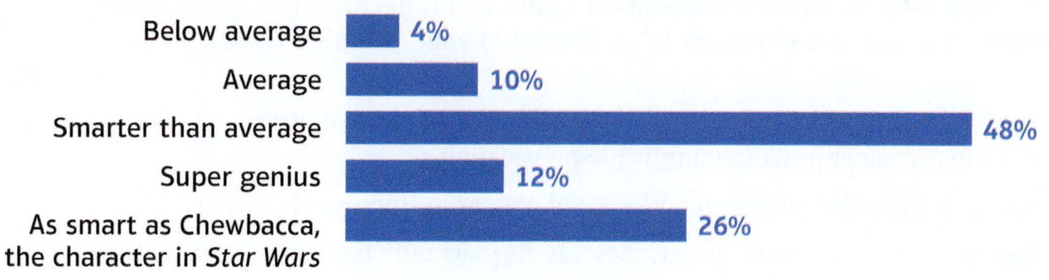

8. **To relax in the evening, I like to**

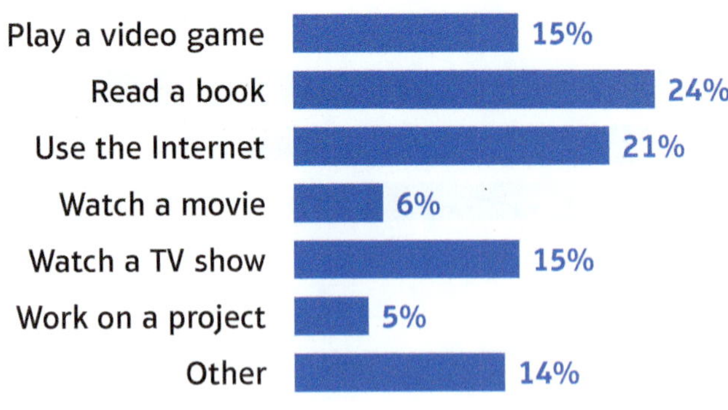

9. **Is your workplace neat or messy?**

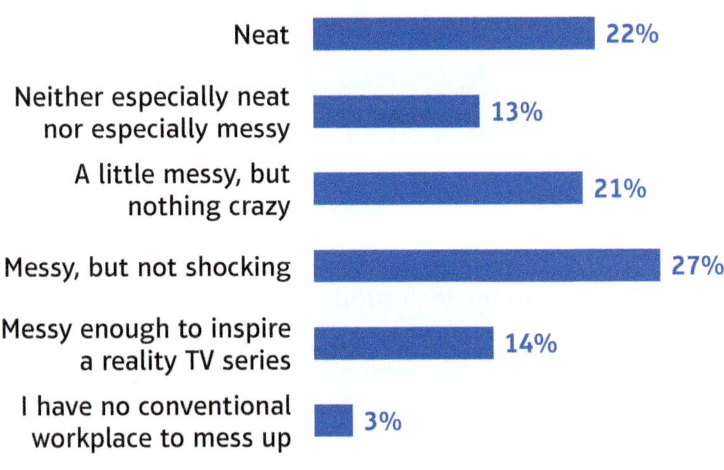

DISCUSSION

A **In a small group, read the statements below about geeks. Try to guess which statements are true and which are false. Check (✓) your group's answers.**

	True	False
1. Some travel companies offer special "Geek Vacations" so that geeks can take classes in computer programming while on vacation.	☐	☐
2. Geeks at some universities can take special classes to improve their social skills.	☐	☐
3. Although many geeks type all day, they say they actually type more slowly than most people they know.	☐	☐
4. An organization called "Girl-Geek Dinners" helps women who are interested in information technology meet one another.	☐	☐
5. "Geek Pride Day" is celebrated annually in many countries.	☐	☐
6. "Geek chic" is a new fashion trend. Men and women who are not actually geeks try to dress the way geeks do.	☐	☐

B **Tell the class your group's answers. Then check the Key on page 131 to find out if your group's answers were correct.**

C **According to Jon Katz, the statements below describe geeks. Read each statement. Check *Yes* if the statement describes you and *No* if it doesn't.**

	Yes	No
1. You are online a good part of the time.	☐	☐
2. You feel a personal connection with technology.	☐	☐
3. You like popular culture (popular movies, music, TV programs).	☐	☐
4. You don't like being told what to do.	☐	☐
5. You believe that people in authority are not on your side.	☐	☐
6. You like to solve problems and puzzles.	☐	☐
7. You love to create things.	☐	☐
8. You see yourself as an outsider—someone who never quite fits in.	☐	☐

D **Discuss the answers to these questions:**

1. Who in the class fits Jon Katz's description of a geek?
2. Who in the class definitely does not fit his description of a geek?
3. Do you think the statements describe only geeks in the United States, or is there an "international geek"? (To find out, you could give the test to people from three different countries. Did some people answer *Yes* often?)

E **Here are some words that people who work in technology fields use. (These expressions, called *techspeak*, might not be in your dictionary.) In a small group, try to guess the meaning of these expressions.**

1. Eye candy	(Hint: Candy is something good to eat, so eye candy must be something good to _______.)
2. Scareware	(Hint: What could be scary about a program you download from the Internet on to your computer?)
3. Treeware	(Hint: What is made from trees?)
4. TLDR	(Hint: You might write this if you don't have time to read a long article or blog post.)
5. UX	(Hint: After you visit a Web site, you might say you had a good—or a bad—UX.)
6. Content farm	(Hint: A farm usually has many different kinds of animals.)

F **When your group has made its decisions, tell the class your guesses. Then check the Key on page 131 to find out if your group was right.**

WRITING

Choose one of the following topics to write about.

1. Jerry Yang is athletic (not a typical geek characteristic) and was popular in high school (not a typical geek characteristic). So, he is described as "not a typical geek." Can anyone really be described as a typical anything? Can you say, for example, that someone is a typical athlete, a typical artist, or a typical American? Explain your answer.
2. Jerry Yang and David Filo's story is called a "rags-to-riches" story. Because of Yahoo!'s success, they went from having no money to having a lot of money. Do you know a rags-to-riches story? Tell the story in writing.
3. Many people who started successful tech companies are philanthropists—they give money and time to make life better for others. Search "philanthropy tech companies" on the Internet to find examples. Write a paragraph about the philanthropy of one person or company.
4. Jon Katz writes that geeks feel a personal connection with technology. What are your feelings about devices and services, such as computers, smartphones, social media, e-mail, and texting? Choose one device or service and explain what you like or don't like about it.
5. Jon Katz believes that it's a great time to be a geek. Is it a great time to be a geek in your country? Explain why it is or isn't.
6. Are you a technology geek? Explain why you are or aren't.
7. The definition of the word *geek* is changing in English. It used to mean someone who knows a lot about computing. Now it can mean someone who knows a lot about any topic. For example, someone could be a history geek, a plant geek, or a book geek. Does the new definition of *geek* fit you? If so, explain what topic you are geeky about.

UNIT 4

Finding the Right Person to Marry

Have you already found the person you want to marry? Or are you still looking for the right person?

A The following statements are about love and marriage. Read each statement. Write *Yes* on the line if you agree with the statement and *No* if you disagree.

_______ 1. "True love" comes to you only once in your lifetime.

_______ 2. "Love at first sight" can happen.

_______ 3. Love between people from different countries is more difficult than love between two people from the same country.

_______ 4. It is very important that your husband or wife is your "soul mate"—your best friend and partner, someone who understands you.

_______ 5. The most important reason to get married is to have children.

_______ 6. It is important for a woman to marry a man who can make enough money to support a family.

_______ 7. It is important to marry someone who shares your religion.

_______ 8. Choosing the person you marry is the most important decision of your life.

B Share your answers with the class. Did your classmates respond to the statements in the same way?

In this unit, you will first read a true story about two people who unexpectedly found love on the Internet. Then you will find out what young adults in the United States are looking for in a spouse.

A TRUE STORY IN THE NEWS

PRE-READING

A **Discuss the answers to these questions with your classmates.**

1. Is online dating a good way to meet people?
2. Does online dating help people find a better match than other ways—for example, through friends or at a party?
3. Have you, or has someone you know, used online dating?
4. Which online dating sites are the best?
5. Have you, or has someone you know, had a bad experience with online dating?
6. Do you know any married couples who met through online dating?

B **When you have finished reading the story, look back at Question 1 above. Would you answer it differently?**

The Real Ronaldo

1 Emma Perrier spent the summer mending a broken heart after a recent breakup. By September, she had grown tired of watching old movies alone in her apartment near London. She decided it was time to forget her ex-boyfriend and start dating again. Despite the horror stories she'd heard about online dating, Emma, 33, downloaded a matchmaking app called Zoosk. The second "o" in the Zoosk logo looked like a diamond engagement ring, which suggested that its 38 million members were looking for serious relationships.

2 Deep down Emma did not believe that computers were the best way to find love, but she felt she had no better options. She worked long hours as the manager of a coffee shop, and she avoided pubs and nightclubs. So she found it difficult to meet men. Emma took the three selfies the app required and posted them.

3 As soon as her dating profile went live, Emma's phone started to bleep with interest from strangers. The app allowed her to gaze at a vast assortment of men like cakes in a coffee-shop window, but not interact with them until she subscribed to the app. She was interested in one man's photos in particular: He was a dark-haired Italian named Ronaldo Scicluna, whose nickname was Ronnie. He was boyish yet mysterious—he looked like the kind of male model she saw in cologne commercials on TV. In her favorite photo, Ronnie wore a leather jacket that made him look like a pop star. But according to his profile, Ronnie was a 34-year-old electrician who lived just 100 miles away. He seemed exciting, so Emma paid the £25 ($34) subscription to Zoosk.

4 An exchange of messages between Emma and Ronnie followed. Emma discovered that she and Ronnie were two lonely Europeans working in England—Emma was from France, and Ronnie was from Italy. Sometimes Ronnie wrote to Emma in French, but when she wrote to him in Italian, she was surprised that he didn't know it. His mother was English, Ronnie explained, and his Italian father spoke English, too. So he had never learned Italian well.

5 One day Ronnie wrote, "You look beautiful. You could easily have picked someone else."

6 "No. You're the only one I wanted to talk to. I paid the subscription because of you," she replied.

7 "As soon as I saw your picture I wanted you," he wrote.

8 "Makes me happy to know that," Emma replied.

9 When four red heart emojis appeared on her screen, Emma was thrilled. Unlike her ex-boyfriend, Ronnie seemed mature and attentive. Ronnie was handsome, funny, and caring, but there was one problem: He did not exist.

10 Ronaldo Scicluna was a fictional character created by a short, balding, 53-year-old man named Alan. His alter ego "Ronnie" was charming and attractive—everything Alan was not. Divorced and lonely, Alan wanted to meet new people, but he lacked self-confidence and feared rejection. Then one day he noticed the online-dating service Zoosk. When he posted his dating profile, he used photos of a male model that he found on the Internet.

11 Emma constantly asked Ronnie to meet in person, but he always made excuses. "I don't think you realize how difficult it is for me to get time off from work," he wrote. "But I love you."

12 "And I love you, too," she replied.

13 Five months after her relationship with Ronnie began, Emma took a new job as the assistant manager of an Italian restaurant in London. One night, after the last customers left the restaurant, Emma was closing up with one of the waiters. As they shut down the huge pizza oven and packed away the silverware, Emma told him about her mysterious long-distance boyfriend. He listened for a while, then turned to Emma and said, "But Emma, the guy doesn't want to meet you. Maybe it's not even him."

14 "But we've talked on the phone," Emma replied.

15 "He's probably an old man," the waiter replied. "Or he could be a psycho."

continued ▶

16 He told her about an app called Reverse Image Search. It searches the Internet to find the original source of a profile picture. One evening after work, Emma downloaded the app and then uploaded the photo of Ronnie wearing his leather jacket. The results arrived in seconds: The man in the photo was a model and actor from Turkey named Adem Guzel.

17 "Do you have anything to tell me about Adem Guzel?" Emma wrote Ronnie in a text message.

18 "It's me," Alan replied, thinking fast. "Those are my modeling pictures. I once used another name. It was a long time ago."

19 Then Alan made his first mistake.

20 In August, nearly a year after his and Emma's relationship began, he bought a new computer and set it up using his personal e-mail address. The next time he sent Emma an e-mail, the name "Alan" was in the e-mail address.

21 "Who's Alan?" Emma wrote him. "I bought the computer from somebody else," Alan lied, "and they didn't change the e-mail address."

22 Emma was now overwhelmed with doubts. She typed Alan's entire e-mail address into Google. She found his Twitter accounts and photos of him—the real him. She called him.

23 "Is your real name Alan?" Emma asked.

24 "No," he answered.

25 "But it is, it is, it is!" Emma said. Finally, Alan told her everything. Then they both cried.

26 Emma decided that she needed to protect others from Alan's scam. She wrote a Facebook message to the Turkish model. "Hello Adem," she wrote. "We don't know each other, but a year ago I met a guy online, and that man is using your picture and pretends he is you under another name. I wasn't sure if getting in touch with you was a good idea, but I needed you to know. Kind regards, Emma."

27 Adem usually didn't write back to strangers who contacted him on Facebook. But something about the sincerity of Emma's message stuck in his mind. He wrote back in English, their common language. That was the beginning of a conversation between Adem and Emma. When Emma asked Adem if he wanted to video call, he said yes.

28 When Adem's face appeared on her phone, Emma began to cry. Until she saw his face, she wasn't sure it was him; she was always in doubt. But there he was, talking, smiling, nervously running his fingers through his hair.

29 "You're real!" Emma said. "You really exist!"

30 For the next four months, Emma and Adem continued their conversation. Incredibly, Emma was once again in a long-distance romance. But this time, she wouldn't be a fool. She invited Adem to visit London so they could meet in person. Adem said yes immediately.

31 Three months later, Emma stood beneath the giant arrivals board at London airport, searching for Adem's flight. When the woman beside her noticed that her hands were shaking, Emma explained that she was waiting for a man she had met on the Internet. The woman froze. "You have to be very careful!" she warned. "On the Internet, not everyone is who they say they are."

32 "Well, actually, I know…" Emma began, but the Turkish passengers were already coming into the arrivals hall. When the crowd parted, she saw Adem walking toward her in a white T-shirt and a blue cardigan—he was the man in the photos, come to life. When Emma shook Adem's hand, she noticed that his hands were shaking, too.

33 For the next few weeks, Emma and Adem explored London together, walking around and taking pictures of themselves with a selfie stick. When Adem wore the leather jacket from her favorite photo, Emma felt starstruck. And Adem couldn't believe his luck—his soul mate had appeared in his inbox as if by magic.

34 One evening during Adem's visit, Emma was closing down the restaurant after a busy shift. Night shifts had always been one of her loneliest times, when she would hope that Ronaldo—"Ronnie"—would materialize from the Internet and walk her home. Of course, Ronaldo had never appeared; he didn't exist. That night she looked up from her work and saw a handsome man standing in the doorway of the restaurant, waiting for her. It was Adem. And he was real.

GETTING THE BIG PICTURE

Imagine this: A friend of Emma's is thinking about trying online dating. She asks Emma, "Should I try it?" What do you think Emma's answer would be?

a. No, definitely not!

b. Yes, definitely!

c. Yes, but be careful.

BUILDING VOCABULARY

RECALLING NEW WORDS

Read each sentence. What is the meaning of the word(s) in *italics*? Write the letter of your answer on the line.

d 1. Emma spent the summer *mending a broken heart.*

____ 2. She thought looking for love on the Internet was her best *option.*

____ 3. When men's photos appeared on her screen, Emma *gazed at them.*

____ 4. The photos showed *a vast assortment* of men.

____ 5. She read Ronnie's *profile.*

____ 6. When four red hearts appeared on her screen, Emma was *thrilled.*

____ 7. "Ronnie" was Alan's *alter ego.*

____ 8. Alan *lacked* self-confidence.

____ 9. Emma *was overwhelmed with* doubts.

____ 10. She wanted to protect others from Alan's *scam.*

____ 11. She wasn't sure if *getting in touch* with Adem was a good idea.

____ 12. When Adem wore the leather jacket from her favorite photo, Emma felt *starstruck.*

a. happy and excited

b. dishonest trick

c. the same admiration she would feel for someone famous

d. trying not to feel sad

e. didn't have

f. looked at them for a long time

g. communicating

h. choice

i. different version of himself

j. many types

k. short description that gave information about him

l. had too many

UNDERSTANDING SPECIALIZED VOCABULARY

Many of the events in the story take place in the online world, not in the physical world. So to understand the story, it is necessary to understand the specialized vocabulary of the Internet.

A Match each Internet word with a definition. Write the letter of your answer on the line.

Internet Word	Definition
____ 1. app	a. picture you take of yourself, usually with a smartphone
____ 2. download	b. small symbol that shows ideas or emotions—for example, happiness or surprise
____ 3. upload	c. move something from a smaller electronic device to a large computer or computer network
____ 4. selfie	d. a computer program that performs a special function
____ 5. post	e. get something ready to use
____ 6. emoji	f. move something from a large computer or computer network to a smaller electronic device—a smartphone, for example
____ 7. set up	g. put something on an Internet page

B If you and your classmates use electronic devices like laptops, tablets, and smartphones, discuss the following questions.

1. What apps have you downloaded? Which one is your favorite?
2. Do you have a favorite selfie? Show it to your classmates.
3. Do you often post on social media? What kinds of things do you post?
4. Do you use emojis? If so, which one do you use most often?
5. When you buy a new electronic device, who sets it up?

DEVELOPING READING SKILLS

UNDERSTANDING THE MAIN IDEAS

Cross out the information that is not in the story. You will cross out one line in each group.

1. Words that describe Emma at the beginning of the story
   a. living in an apartment near London
   b. from France
   c. recovering from a recent break-up
   d. coffee-shop manager
   e. reading mystery novels
   f. 33 years old

2. What Emma did after downloading a matchmaking app
   a. took three selfies and posted them
   b. looked at photos of men
   c. contacted three men
   d. paid the subscription
3. How "Ronnie" described himself
   a. full name Ronaldo Scicluna
   b. electrician
   c. boat owner
   d. living 100 miles from Emma
   e. from Italy
   f. 34 years old
4. Words that describe Alan
   a. short and balding
   b. loved to travel
   c. 53 years old
   d. divorced
   e. lacked self-confidence
5. Words that describe Adem
   a. model and actor
   b. from Turkey
   c. dark-haired
   d. mysterious-looking
   e. sometimes used matchmaking apps
   f. didn't usually write to strangers on Facebook
6. What the waiter at the restaurant told Emma
   a. "Ronnie" doesn't want to meet you.
   b. He's probably an old man.
   c. Maybe he's married.
   d. He could be a psycho.
7. Clues that "Ronnie" wasn't who he said he was
   a. He said he was from Italy, but he didn't know Italian.
   b. He said he was too busy to meet Emma in person.
   c. He sent a text message that said, "Love you, Alan."
   d. An app identified him in a photo as Adem Gunzel.
   e. His e-mail address said "Alan."

UNDERSTANDING CAUSE AND EFFECT

Complete each sentence with information from the story. Write your answer on the line. There may be several correct ways to complete each sentence.

1. Emma found it difficult to meet men because ______________________________

______________________________.

2. Emma was interested in meeting Ronaldo because ______________________________

______________________________.

3. "Ronnie" said he had never learned Italian well because ______________________________

______________________________.

4. Alan used someone else's photo with his dating profile because ______________________________

______________________________.

5. Alan said his e-mail address said "Alan" because ______________________________

______________________________.

6. Emma wrote a Facebook message to Adem because ______________________________

______________________________.

SUMMARIZING

> *Summarizing* is a good way to check your comprehension. When you write a summary, you include only the main information and not the details. A summary is shorter than the original reading.

While Emma was waiting for Adem's plane at the London airport, she had a short conversation with a woman who was also standing under the arrivals board. When Emma told her that she was waiting for someone she had met on the Internet, the woman said, "You have to be very careful! On the Internet, not everyone is who they say they are."

"Well, actually, I know…" Emma began. Then Adem arrived, and Emma and the woman never finished their conversation.

Imagine this: Adem's plane was delayed several hours. The plane the woman was waiting for was delayed several hours, too. So the conversation between Emma and the woman continued. Emma told the woman how she met Adem. On a separate piece of paper, write what Emma said. Include only the main information and not the details. You could begin this way:

Well, actually, I know. I subscribed to a dating app, and I met a man who said his name was Ronaldo.

NEWS AND VIEWS

In the story "The Real Ronaldo," you read that "Ronnie" had many of the qualities that Emma was looking for. He was mature, attentive, funny, caring, and attractive. Now you will learn what most young adults in the United States are looking for in a husband or wife. The information comes from a survey done by the National Marriage Project, a group that studies the health of marriage in the United States.

A **Before you read the article, try to predict what the survey showed. Read each statement below. Write *Yes* on the line if you agree with the statement and *No* if you disagree.**

_______ 1. Young adults in the United States are probably looking for the same qualities Emma was looking for.

_______ 2. They are probably looking for the same qualities their parents and grandparents were looking for.

_______ 3. They are probably looking for the same qualities I am (or was) looking for.

B **Now read the article to find out what the survey actually showed.**

Who Wants to Marry a Soul Mate?

1 What are young adults in the United States looking for in a spouse? Are they looking for a person who will be a great father or mother someday? No. Are they looking for someone who will help them financially? No. Are they looking for someone who shares their religion? Most say no. What, then, are they looking for in a husband or wife? They are looking for someone who is, above all, their "soul mate"—someone who is their best friend and partner, someone who understands them, someone with whom they have a deep emotional connection.

2 That information comes from a telephone survey of 1,000 Americans ages 20 to 29. Researchers with the National Marriage Project called young men and women living in the eastern United States and read statements about marriage. After each statement, the young adults in the study replied "yes" if they agreed and "no" if they disagreed. Here, for example, are a few of the statements:

- The main purpose of marriage is to have children.
- A woman should not rely on marriage for financial security.
- It is important to find a spouse who shares your religion.

To the surprise of the researchers, the statement receiving the largest percentage of "yes" responses, with 94 percent agreeing, was: "When you marry, you want your spouse to be your soul mate, first and foremost."

3 Sociologists say these results indicate that in the United States young adults' attitudes toward marriage are different from those of their grandparents and great-grandparents. Many of the social, economic, and religious reasons for marrying and choosing a spouse that were important to previous generations are no longer important. In the past, for example, many people

continued ▶

believed the purpose of marriage was to have children—to create a family. Only 16 percent of young adults questioned in the survey believe that "the main purpose of marriage is to have children." In earlier generations, most women saw marriage as a way to become economically independent from their parents and financially secure. Today, a young woman is more likely to rely on herself financially, believing that her own education and career—not her husband's—will give her economic independence and security. Not long ago, most people in the United States thought it was very important to marry someone of the same religion. Today, only 42 percent of young adults believe this.

4 Replacing yesterday's social, economic, and religious reasons for marrying are reasons that are romantic, perhaps even naive or unrealistic. Today's young adults want, more than anything else, to have togetherness, support, and closeness in their marriages; they want a "super-relationship" between two people, rather than a relationship that is just one of many close relationships they have.

5 Some sociologists believe that young people in the United States may be looking for this "super-relationship" because they do not have many other relationships that are strong and lasting. Contemporary U.S. society is mobile—many people move as often as every seven years—and the pace of life is frantic. Those two factors make it difficult to have deep and lasting relationships. In addition, the divorce rate is high in the United States; 43 percent of all marriages end. So, young adults may be looking for the emotional support and comfort that is missing from other parts of their lives.

6 Hayley Kaufman, a reporter at the *Boston Globe* who is in her late 20s, agrees that the high divorce rate may explain her generation's search for a soul mate. In a *Boston Globe* article, she writes:

> 7 While the soul-mate idea may have older Americans shaking their heads and laughing, it makes perfect sense to those of us who are in our twenties and thirties. We're the ones, after all, who watched our parents split up and our friends' parents split up.
>
> 8 By the mid-1980s, as the American divorce rate was peaking at 50 percent, our lives had been marked by events our parents never could have dreamed of when they were kids. We sat through family-therapy sessions before getting dropped off at school puffy-eyed and sniffling. We woke up one morning to discover that Dad had packed a suitcase and moved into an apartment. At the tender age of 10, we carried around two different sets of house keys—one set for Mom's house, another set for Dad's.
>
> 9 Even if our parents decided to stick it out, many of our friends' parents didn't. We watched as parent after parent moved out and, frequently, remarried. We were the ones who got the phone calls after our depressed, angry, and just plain sad adolescent friends had just eaten a holiday dinner with a bunch of steprelatives they barely knew.
>
> 10 The people we saw split up weren't soul mates—not by a long shot. Surely they'd been in love at some point. But they got married for a lot of other reasons. They wanted a provider. Or someone who shared the same religion. Or a good mother for their kids. Or they thought it was just time.
>
> 11 It's no wonder young Americans want a soul mate. After a lifetime of broken bonds, we're all hoping for one relationship that will last.

12 The survey seems to support Ms. Kaufman's belief that her generation is looking for "one relationship that will last." When researchers read this statement: "It is unlikely that I will stay married to the same person for life," only 6 percent of young adults agreed. In other words, 94 percent of the people who participated in the survey intend to stay married to their "soul mates" for their entire lives.

13 Older adults—even the ones shaking their heads and laughing at the "soul mate" idea—wish them well and hope they do.

BUILDING ACADEMIC VOCABULARY

The words below are on the Academic Word List. Find the words in "Who Wants to Marry a Soul Mate?" (The number in parentheses is the number of the paragraph.) If you are not sure what a word means, look it up in your dictionary. Then use the words in the sentences that follow.

financially (1)	previous (3)	created (3)	bond (11)
attitude (3)	generations (3)	secure (3)	participated (12)
economic (3)	rely on (3)		

1. Some people believe that the universe began with a big explosion, but others do not believe it was ___created___ in that way.
2. If your car always starts and never breaks down, you have a car you can __________________.
3. A photo of a woman with her daughter, granddaughter, and great-granddaughter shows four __________________ in a family.
4. Most job applications ask for information about work experience you've had. You usually have to list all your __________________ employers.
5. He has a close relationship with his cousin, but the __________________ with his brother is even stronger.
6. When she was in high school, she played soccer and belonged to several clubs; all together, she __________________ in four after-school activities.
7. Small children stay close to their parents, where they feel safe and __________________.
8. Students who hated school, but like it now, had a change in __________________.
9. Someone who loans you money helps you out __________________.
10. If a country's unemployment rate is high—that is, if a lot of people can't find work—the country's __________________ situation is not good.

DEVELOPING READING SKILLS

UNDERSTANDING THE MAIN IDEAS

There are three correct ways to complete each sentence. Cross out the one incorrect answer.

1. A recent survey indicates that young adults in the United States want to marry a "soul mate." A soul mate is someone
   a. with whom you have a deep emotional connection.
   b. who understands you.
   c. ~~who will help you financially.~~
   d. who is your best friend and partner.

2. The survey was conducted in this way:
   a. Researchers with the National Marriage Project telephoned 1,000 Americans ages 20 to 29.
   b. The researchers read statements about marriage.
   c. The young adults responded "yes" if they agreed with the statement and "no" if they disagreed.
   d. The researchers asked the young adults to describe what they were looking for in a spouse.

3. In the past, many people believed that
   a. the purpose of marriage was to have children.
   b. marriage was a way for a woman to become financially secure.
   c. it was very important to marry someone of the same religion.
   d. marriage was hard work and a full-time job.

4. Some young adults in the United States do not have many deep and lasting relationships because
   a. in the United States, work is more important than friends and family.
   b. people move often, making it difficult to make friends.
   c. the frantic pace of life leaves no time for friends.
   d. family members become separated when parents divorce.

5. Hayley Kaufman, a reporter at the *Boston Globe*, writes that
   a. the divorce rate was at 50 percent when she was growing up.
   b. many couples in her parents' generation married not for love but for other reasons.
   c. the "soul mate" idea makes perfect sense to her generation.
   d. she has already found her soul mate.

SEPARATING FACT FROM OPINION

The ability to separate a fact from an opinion is an important reading skill. A *fact* is information that is known to be true or can be proven. For example, this statement is a fact: "In the United States, the average age for men to marry is 29, and for women it is 27." An *opinion* is a person's ideas or beliefs and cannot be proven. This statement is an opinion: "Men should not get married until they are at least 25 years old."

Read the following sentences from the article. If you think the sentence gives you a fact, write *F* on the line. If you think the sentence gives you an opinion, write *O* on the line.

F 1. Researchers with the National Marriage Project conducted a telephone survey of 1,000 Americans ages 20 to 29.

____ 2. It is important to find a spouse who shares your religion.

____ 3. The main purpose of marriage is to have children—to create a family.

____ 4. Ninety-four percent of the people who participated in the survey say they want their spouse to be their soul mate.

____ 5. A woman should not rely on marriage for financial security.

____ 6. Young adults in the United States want to marry for reasons that are romantic—perhaps even naive or unrealistic.

____ 7. Contemporary U.S. society is mobile: Many people move as often as every seven years.

____ 8. In the mid-1980s, the American divorce rate was peaking at 50 percent.

READING A BAR GRAPH

You learned in the article "Who Wants to Marry a Soul Mate?" that researchers telephoned people in the United States ages 20 to 29 to find out what they thought about marriage. Below are some statements from the survey and the percentages of people agreeing with them. The percentages are presented in a bar graph.

A **Respond to the survey. Read each statement. Write *Yes* on the line if you agree with the statement and *No* if you disagree. (If you are already married, answer the questions as you would have answered them before you were married.) Then look at the bar graph to see how your opinions compare with the opinions of the people who participated in the survey.**

Survey of Beliefs about Marriage

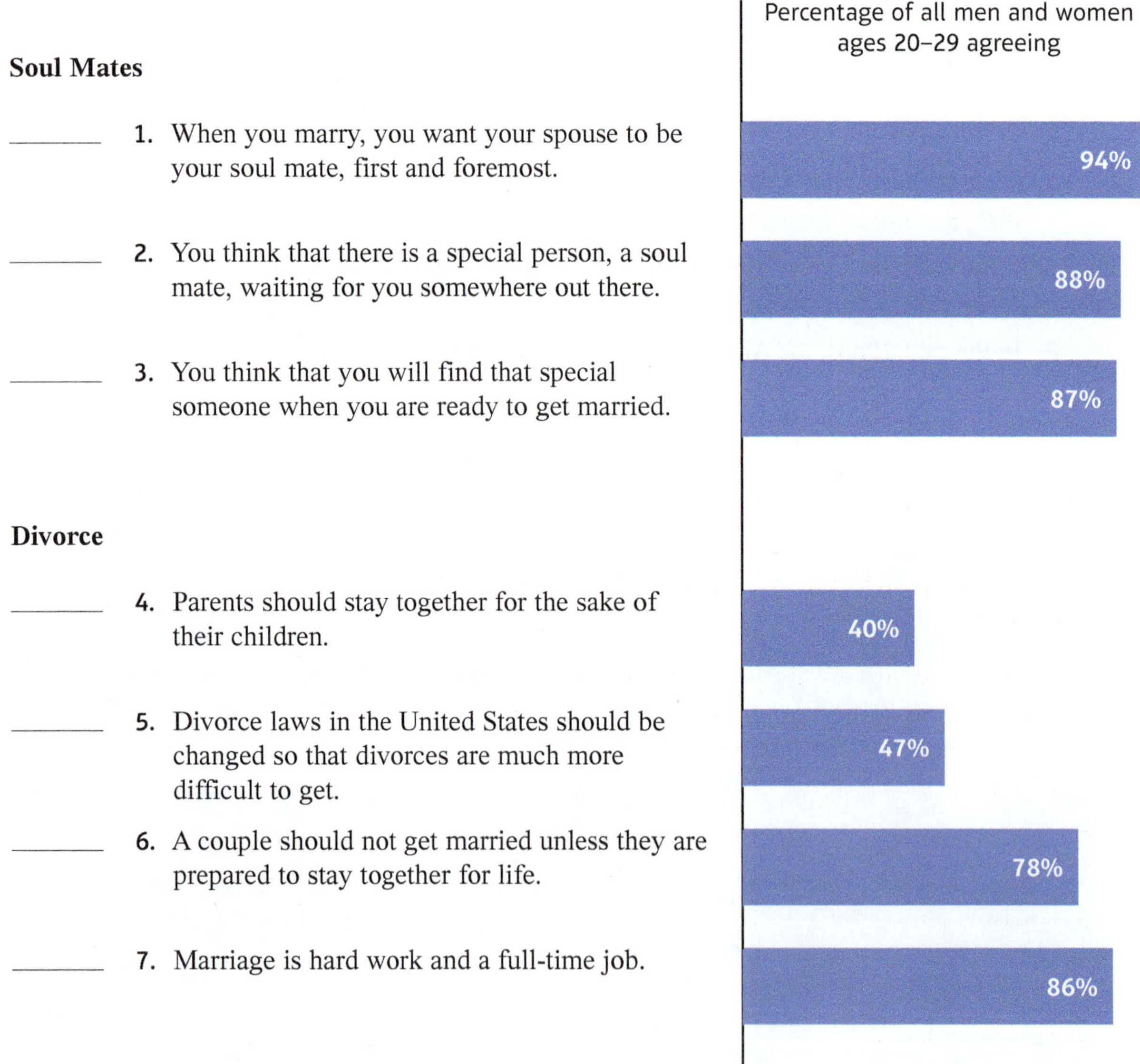

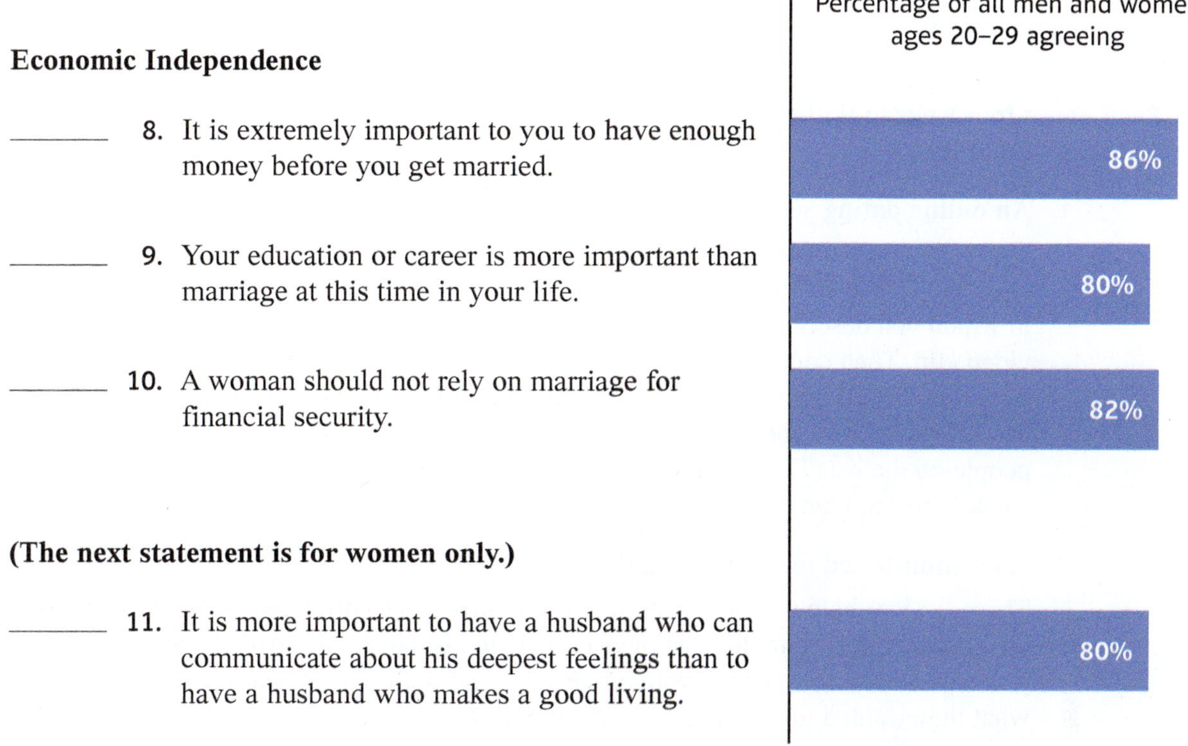

Economic Independence

_______ 8. It is extremely important to you to have enough money before you get married.

_______ 9. Your education or career is more important than marriage at this time in your life.

_______ 10. A woman should not rely on marriage for financial security.

(The next statement is for women only.)

_______ 11. It is more important to have a husband who can communicate about his deepest feelings than to have a husband who makes a good living.

B **Discuss the answers to these questions with your classmates.**

1. Compare your answers to the survey with those of a classmate. Which of your answers are the same? Which are different? Explain why you answered the way you did.
2. Do you think young adults in your native country would give the same answers that young adults in the United States did? Circle the statements you think young people in your native country would answer very differently. Show the statements you circled to a classmate from a different country. Did you circle the same statements?

C **Use the statements from the survey in A to conduct your own survey. Follow the steps below.**

1. First, decide who will participate in your survey. For example, you could survey a group of other students from your country. If you decide to survey people who are already married, you will need to change or omit some of the statements.
2. Conduct the survey as the researchers did, asking people to respond "yes" if they agree with the statements and "no" if they disagree.
3. Record the results of your survey as percentages. Compare the results of your survey with the results of the survey in A. You can summarize your results in an oral report, in a short essay, or in a bar graph.

DISCUSSION

A **Read about four ways to find a soul mate and rate them with 1 to 4 stars. (Four stars = You think it's a great idea.)**

_________ 1. **An online dating service**

There are approximately 8,000 Web sites worldwide that help people find love on the Internet. This is how most of the Web sites work: First, you fill out a questionnaire in which you describe yourself. You might also include a photo of yourself or a short video clip. Then computers search for people who might be a good match for you—someone, for example, who shares your religion, race, values, or interests. The online dating service then sends you a list of possible matches. It is up to you to contact the people on the list. There is a monthly fee for online dating services, although the first week is free at many sites.

_________ 2. **A location-based matchmaking device**

These devices help two strangers near each other meet—strangers on a city street or on a subway, for example. One device, invented in Japan, was called Lovegety. It was a plastic gadget people wore around their necks. Lovegetys asked their owners what they wanted to do: have fun, dance, fall in love, see a movie, chat, or meet for a drink. The owners pressed a button to give their answers. When a woman wearing a Lovegety passed a man wearing a Lovegety, the Lovegetys beeped if the two people had chosen the same answers. It was up to the people wearing the beeping Lovegetys to introduce themselves and make a date to meet again. Lovegety was the first device that helped strangers meet this way. Other companies now sell similar products.

_________ 3. **Speed dating**

Speed dating began in Los Angeles. The idea spread across the United States and then around the world—to Canada, to Britain, to the Ukraine, and to Australia. The evening begins with an equal number of men and women pairing off to chat for exactly eight minutes. When a bell rings, everyone moves to a different chair to talk to another person for exactly eight minutes. At the end of the evening, men and women tell the organizers which people they would like to see again, and, if both sides agree, phone numbers are given out.

_________ 4. **Coffee shop dating**

At a café in New York City, you can find more than coffee—you might be able to find romance. Here's how it works: When you order your coffee, the barista will ask you if you are single and interested in meeting someone. If you answer *yes* to both questions, the barista will take your photo and upload it on a tablet. Then you give the barista your e-mail address. You look through the database of other single people who stopped by the café, and if someone interests you, the barista connects you with that person. There is a small charge for each connection the barista makes. The café's owner says, "The idea is to get local people offline and actually meeting, even if it's for a quick 20-minute coffee."

B **Compare your ratings with those of your classmates. Explain why you gave each idea the rating you did. Would you consider trying any of these ways to find a soul mate? If so, which ones?**

C What do you think of this way to find a soul mate? Read this true story about a man named Tom.

Tom was experimenting with a computer program. The program lets people select facial features—a nose, eyes, a mouth, a chin—and puts them together to create a picture of a person. Just for fun, Tom decided to create the face of his "dream girl." Tom's problem is that he fell in love with the face he created. Using the Internet, he is trying to find a woman who looks like his "dream girl." Look at the picture and read the message he posted:

Have you seen this girl?

My name is Tom Kraemer. I created the picture of the girl above on a computer. She does not actually exist. Since creating the picture, I have fallen in love with the girl in the image. Perhaps this doesn't make sense to you, but I believe I have created the image of my soul mate. She is my "dream girl." I know this might sound strange, but I have to find the girl who matches this image. I know my dream girl, my soul mate, is out there somewhere. Have you seen her? Do you know her? PLEASE have her contact me. My happiness depends on it. Thank you.

D Discuss the answers to these questions with your classmates.

1. What do you think are Tom's chances of finding a woman who looks like the one in the picture? (Check the Key on page 131 to read about his progress so far.)
2. If Tom finds his "dream girl," what do you think their chances are for being happy together?
3. After Tom created the picture of his "dream girl," he fell in love with her. Do you believe in love at first sight? Has it happened to you or to someone you know? Tell the class the story.
4. Tom knows exactly what he wants his soul mate to look like. What about you? Are you attracted to a person who looks a certain way—to someone who is tall, for example, or who has a big smile? Look on the Internet for photos of people who are your "dream men" or "dream women." Show the photos to your classmates and explain why you chose the photos you did.

5. Tom is looking for a soul mate who looks like the picture. Do you think looks are important in finding a soul mate? What other qualities are important? With your classmates, make a list of important qualities. Write your list on the board.
6. Separate into two groups, men and women. The women will go to one room, and the men will go to another room. From the list of qualities you and your classmates wrote on the board, each group will choose the five qualities they think are most important in choosing a spouse. Then the groups will come back together. Did the men and women choose the same qualities? If not, why do you think they didn't?

WRITING

Choose one of the following topics to write about.

1. Do you want your spouse to be your soul mate, first and foremost? Explain your answer.
2. Re-read the statements in the survey on pages 64–65. Find a statement with which you strongly agree, or find a statement with which you strongly disagree. Explain why you agree or disagree with the statement.
3. At matchmaking Web sites, people try to find love on the Internet. Some sites have a list of questions. The first questions are basic—for example: What is your gender? Height? Religion? Occupation? The next questions require a little more thought. Below are examples of some of those questions. Choose one of the questions and answer it.
   - How would your best friend describe you?
   - What do you like to do for fun?
   - When are you the happiest?
   - What are three things you're thankful for?
   - What are you proud of?
   - What's your idea of a perfect date?
   - What do you think you'll be doing five years from now?

UNIT 5

Intuition

The theme of this unit is intuition. Intuition is the ability to know something or understand something by using your feelings instead of carefully considering all the facts. Researcher William Kautz developed the quiz below to help people find out how often they use their intuition.

A **Answer each question by putting a check (✓) in the box.**

	Never	Rarely	Sometimes	Frequently
1. When the doorbell or phone rings unexpectedly, do you know who is there?	☐	☐	☐	☐
2. Have you ever thought about someone you haven't thought of for months and then received an e-mail or a phone call from that person?	☐	☐	☐	☐
3. Do you ever dream about unusual events that actually occur later?	☐	☐	☐	☐
4. Have you ever made a mistake and later realized you had sensed at that time it wasn't the right thing to do?	☐	☐	☐	☐
5. Do your first impressions of people turn out to be accurate?	☐	☐	☐	☐

B **Score your quiz.**

Give yourself: **0 points** for each time you checked *Never*
1 point for each time you checked *Rarely*
2 points for each time you checked *Sometimes*
3 points for each time you checked *Frequently*

Add up your points. **0–5 points** = You rarely use your intuition; **6–10 points** = You sometimes use your intuition; **11–15 points** = You use your intuition often.

In this unit, you will read about a woman whose intuition led her to an important scientific discovery. Then you will learn how psychologists define intuition and how you can learn to use your own intuition.

A TRUE STORY IN THE NEWS

Sue Hendrickson

PRE-READING

A **Look at the photo and think about these questions. Discuss your answers with your classmates.**

1. Do you know anything about the skeleton in the photo?
2. Who could the woman in the photo be?
3. The story on the next page is about the discovery of an important skeleton, and the theme of this unit is "intuition." How could the discovery of a skeleton have anything to do with intuition? What is your guess?

B **Now read the story to find out if you guessed correctly.**

A Sixth Sense

1 Because of a flat tire, Sue Hendrickson found the bones that made her famous.

2 Sue Hendrickson was with a small group of fossil hunters in South Dakota. They had been digging for dinosaur bones all summer, and the dig had been productive. But now it was time to pack up camp and head home. Then, two days before they planned on leaving, the team woke up to find one of the tires on their truck flat and the spare tire low on air. Sue's colleagues headed to a repair station in town, and she stayed behind to continue packing. As she worked, she kept thinking about a small cliff she had seen while exploring nearby ranchland earlier that summer. Her intuition had told her to take a closer look at the cliff, but she hadn't found time to do it. This was her last chance.

3 Sue and her dog, a golden retriever named Gypsy, took an eight-mile (13 kilometers) walk to the cliff. Sue started looking around its base, and within minutes she spotted some pieces of bone. "Because the bone pieces seemed to have fallen from above, I looked up," Sue says. "About eight feet (2.5 meters) up the cliff face, three vertebrae were sticking out of the dirt. They were huge—each was the size of a dinner plate. By their shape, I knew the bones had come from a meat-eating dinosaur. And by their size, I knew it could only be a Tyrannosaurus rex—the rarest of all dinosaurs. I started to cry—I was very emotional."

4 For the next three weeks, the team worked 14-hour days digging out the dinosaur skeleton, which they named "Sue" in honor of its discoverer. "Sue" turned out to be the most complete Tyrannosaurus skeleton ever found—and the most valuable. After a long court battle, it was ultimately sold at auction for over $8 million.

5 Scientists were not surprised when they learned that Sue Hendrickson had discovered the 67-million-year-old bones. She is famous in the scientific world for having a sixth sense—an almost supernatural ability to find amazing things. She has discovered precious 23-million-year-old butterflies, sunken ships holding Ming Dynasty vases, Napoleon's sunken warships, and Cleopatra's palace, which was submerged in water near Egypt. She has found treasure chests of gold.

6 Even as a child, Sue had a talent for finding things. "I was always walking with my head down," she says. "I'd go up and down the streets near my house, looking for treasure. I even went through garbage cans looking for stuff."

7 Sue was very bright, but she quit high school when she was 17 to see what was beyond the limits of her small hometown. She traveled around the United States for years, supporting herself with whatever work she could find. In Maine, she got a job diving for lobsters, and she discovered she was good at finding them. ("I could think like a lobster," she says.) In Florida, she found work diving with two men who collected tropical fish professionally. She discovered she was good at that, too. From diving for lobsters and tropical fish, she went to diving for sunken ships.

8 In the mid-1970s, Sue was diving for shipwrecks in the Dominican Republic when some friends invited her to go on a day trip to visit an amber mine in the mountains. She decided to go. "A miner showed me an insect preserved in amber," she recalls. "I was fascinated. It looked like it had just been put in the amber, yet it was 23 million years old. That was my introduction to fossils."

9 Amber, which is often used to make jewelry, is tree sap that hardened millions of years ago. Sometimes the sap covered insects when it hardened and preserved them perfectly. The trapped insects are highly valued by scientists, museums, and private collectors. Sue Hendrickson became one of the world's leading suppliers of insects encased in amber. She learned how to tell rare from common insects and traveled often to the Dominican Republic and Mexico. Just as she had been good at finding lobsters and tropical fish, Sue was good at finding rare insects in the amber. Her most important discoveries were three perfect 23-million-year-old butterflies—half of the world's total collection.

continued ▶

10 The scientists Sue met through the amber trade recognized that she had a sixth sense for finding things, and they encouraged her to join them on digs for dinosaur bones. She spent the next six summers looking for dinosaur bones in the American West, and in 1990, she discovered "Sue."

11 What made that Tyrannosaurus rex so incredible? Sue explains, "Most plant-eating dinosaurs ran in herds, like buffalo. Their bones are easy to find if you know where to look. They look like little bits of popcorn all over the place. The T-rexes, who hunted the plant-eaters, traveled alone or in small groups. You never find them." By 1990, fossil hunters had found only 20 T-rex skeletons, and they were at most only 60 percent complete. "Sue" was 90 percent complete—the only bones missing were part of the left leg and a few bones around the neck—so the skeleton gave scientists their first opportunity to see what the Tyrannosaurus rexes were really like. For one thing, scientists learned they were huge; "Sue" is 13 feet (4 meters) tall and 142 feet (12.8 meters) long from her head to the tip of her tail.

12 When she left South Dakota, Sue gave the T-rex skeleton to one of her colleagues, a fossil hunter named Peter Larson. Peter and Sue had been in love, but the romance had ended; the skeleton, Sue says, was a "breaking up" present. Peter intended to put the skeleton in a small private museum in South Dakota. That was not to be.

13 The rancher who owned the land where "Sue" was found claimed the skeleton belonged to him. Then the U.S. government stepped in and claimed it belonged to the people of the United States. For five years, Peter, the rancher, and the U.S. government fought in court over "Sue." Finally, a judge decided that it belonged to the rancher, who immediately announced he would sell it to the highest bidder. The auction took place in New York City in 1997. The Field Museum of Chicago (with money donated by two corporations, McDonald's and Disney) paid $8.3 million for "Sue"—the highest price ever paid for a fossil.

14 Sue Hendrickson never made a penny from the fossil named after her, and that was all right with her. "It's the thrill of discovery, not the money, that excites me," she says. "Finding is the thing."

15 And why, exactly, is Sue so good at finding things? For one thing, she does her homework. Before she goes on a dig or dive, she reads everything she can; she becomes an expert. But the world is full of experts. Why aren't they making the amazing discoveries that Sue has? Some scientists say Sue Hendrickson has a sixth sense; others call it intuition. She just calls her talent "inexplicable." When writer Kathy Passero asked Sue Hendrickson about finding the Tyrannosaurus rex, she said, "I know it sounds crazy to say a 67-million-year-old dinosaur called to me, but it did. It was like a magnetic pull."

GETTING THE BIG PICTURE

Why is Sue Hendrickson famous in the scientific world? Circle the letter of your answer.

a. She discovered the only Tyrannosaurus rex skeleton ever found.

b. She has a talent for finding amazing things—a talent that even she cannot explain.

c. She is one of only a few experts on the dinosaur Tyrannosaurus rex.

BUILDING VOCABULARY

RECALLING NEW WORDS

The words below are from the story. Complete each sentence with the correct word or words.

a sixth sense	donated	inexplicable	thrill
cliff	fossils	rare	vertebrae
colleagues	herds		

1. Sue Hendrickson was with a group of scientists who were looking for ______fossils______; they were especially interested in finding dinosaur bones.
2. The people with whom Sue worked went to get a flat tire repaired. While her __________________ were gone, Sue continued packing.
3. Earlier that summer, Sue had seen a hill with a high, flat side. She decided to go back to explore the __________________.
4. Because of their size and shape, Sue knew that the three __________________ she discovered were from the backbone of a Tyrannosaurus rex.
5. By 1990, only 20 T-rex skeletons had been found; they are __________________.
6. Meat-eating dinosaurs hunted alone or in small groups, whereas plant-eating dinosaurs ran in __________________.
7. The Field Museum of Chicago was able to pay over $8 million for the skeleton because two corporations, McDonald's and Disney, __________________ money to the museum.
8. Sue Hendrickson has an almost supernatural ability that some people call intuition and some call __________________.
9. Sue can't explain why she is so good at finding things; she says her talent is __________________.
10. Sue Hendrickson says that money does not excite her; it is the __________________ of discovering things that excites her.

UNDERSTANDING SPECIAL EXPRESSIONS

Complete the sentences to show that you understand the meanings of the new words. There may be several correct ways to complete each sentence.

1. ***to turn out to be* = to happen in the end (What happened is often not expected.)**

   Example: We thought the party would be boring, but it turned out to be great ______________________________.

   a. The T-rex skeleton that Sue Hendrickson discovered turned out to be ______________________________.

   b. We thought the car would be cheap, but with power seats and anti-lock brakes, it turned out to be ______________________________.

   c. They didn't like each other when they first met, but they turned out to be ______________________________.

2. ***to tell* ______ *from* ______ = to see the difference between two things**

   Example: They are identical twins; even their parents can't tell one from the other.

   a. Sue became one of the world's leading suppliers of insects encased in amber, but first she had to learn to tell ______________ from ______________.

   b. Experts in diamonds can tell ______________ from ______________.

   c. People who pick and eat wild mushrooms can tell ______________ from ______________.

DEVELOPING READING SKILLS

UNDERSTANDING THE MAIN IDEAS

Imagine this: One of your friends is looking at the photo on page 70 and asks you questions about it. Answer each question in a few sentences. Write your answers on the lines.

1. Your friend points to the skeleton and asks, "What's that?" You say:

   ____

   ____

   ____

2. Next, your friend points to Sue Hendrickson and asks, "Who's she?" You say:

____

____

____

3. Finally, your friend points to the title of the story, "A Sixth Sense," and asks, "What does that mean?" You say:

____

____

____

SCANNING FOR INFORMATION

> *Scanning* is reading quickly to find specific information. If, for example, you wanted to know the year in which the dinosaur skeleton was sold at auction, you could scan the story for the information. You would move your eyes quickly across the pages, looking for numbers and dates, until you found "1997"—the information you wanted.

Read the list below. Then scan the story to find which six discoveries Sue Hendrickson made. Cross out the two discoveries she did not make.

1. Napoleon's warships
2. the sunken ship *Titanic*
3. the most complete T-rex skeleton ever found
4. Ming Dynasty vases
5. 23-million-year-old butterflies preserved in amber
6. Cleopatra's palace
7. an ancient Indian village in Mesa Verde, Colorado
8. treasure chests of gold

UNDERSTANDING CHRONOLOGICAL ORDER

Events in a story are usually in chronological order—that is, in the order in which they happened—but sometimes they are not. When they are not, look for phrases that help you understand the chronological order of events (for example, "in 1990" or "when she was 17").

Imagine this: Sue Hendrickson took the photos below. Put the photos in chronological order. Write *1* beneath the photo Sue took first, *2* beneath the photo she took second, *3* beneath the photo she took third, and *4* beneath the photo she took last.

a. _____

b. _____

c. _____

d. _____

NEWS AND VIEWS

Sue Hendrickson's intuition led her to "Sue," one of the most important fossils found in the 20th century. What exactly is intuition? Is it a supernatural power that only a few people have? Or is it something that all of us have? In the article below, psychologists explain what they think intuition is and how best to use it.

Before you read, think about the title of the story: "When Not to Use Your Head." To "use your head" is to think about something in a logical and practical way. When could it possibly be a good idea not to think logically?

When Not to Use Your Head

1 At one time or another, probably everyone has had the feeling that something just wasn't right. Perhaps your body sent you a signal: Your neck muscles tightened, or your stomach went into a knot. Maybe a dream seemed to be warning you of danger. Or maybe you were simply becoming increasingly uncomfortable but couldn't explain why. Probably everyone has had the opposite feeling as well: You just knew that something was right and that everything would turn out fine. Some call these feelings hunches, gut feelings, or a sixth sense. Experts call them intuition.

2 Whatever it is called, this knowledge that seems to come out of nowhere has always fascinated people. What exactly is intuition? And how can we use it?

3 Malcolm Westcott was a professor of psychology in Toronto, Canada, and a leading researcher in the field of intuition. Dr. Westcott noticed that some people seemed to be exceptionally good at solving problems, and he wondered why. To find out, he did this experiment: He gave people problems to solve but did not give them all the information they needed to solve the problems. All of the people in the experiment had to guess at the answers, and most guessed wrong. But a small number of people tended to guess right. What did they do that the others didn't? Apparently they took the little information Dr. Westcott gave them, combined it with bits of knowledge from their own experience, and came up with the right answers.

4 According to Dr. Westcott, this knowledge and experience we carry inside is a key component of intuition. Throughout our lives, we are constantly making complex decisions using the knowledge and experience we have acquired, and we use this knowledge and experience unconsciously—without even knowing we are using it.

5 Consider his example: You hear a loud rumbling noise coming from somewhere beneath your car every time you accelerate. So you take your car in for repair. An inexperienced mechanic might spend hours eliminating each possible cause of the rumble before finding the problem. An experienced mechanic, on the other hand, might take your car out for a five-minute ride, guess what the problem is, and turn out to be right. He could probably not explain how he figured it out so quickly.

6 People like the experienced mechanic sometimes draw on their deep knowledge of problems rather than consciously go through a series of logical steps. Through experience, their hunches keep getting better and better.

7 Many successful people in science, business, the arts, and sports admit that their success is due in part to their intuition. Einstein said, "I believe in intuitions and inspirations," and businessman Ray Kroc said he owed his phenomenal success in part to his intuition. In 1961, Kroc wanted to buy a small chain of

continued ▶

hamburger-and-milkshake restaurants owned by two brothers named McDonald. The McDonald brothers wanted $2.7 million to close the deal. It was an exorbitant price at that time, and Kroc didn't have that kind of money. He borrowed the money and went ahead anyway because he had a feeling in "his bones." We all know the ending to that story.

8 How can you use your intuition to solve problems, make discoveries, and make better decisions? Writer Paul Bagne interviewed several psychologists considered experts in intuition. He talked to them about using intuition and asked them for advice. Here are some tips the experts gave him:

9 ***1. Don't confuse intuition with guessing.*** Real intuition is not just a guess; it has a lot of information behind it. Let's say, for example, that you suddenly have an uneasy feeling boarding an airplane. Do you have information and experience that support your uneasy feeling? Is it statistically likely that the plane will crash? Or are you simply afraid of flying? You might be listening to your fear and not to your intuition.

10 ***2. To use your intuition, first relax.*** When trying to make a decision or solve a problem, we sometimes get confused and overwhelmed by all the facts. Experts say that's the time to back off. Go for a walk, work in your garden, visit a friend, or see a movie. It doesn't matter what you do to relax, as long as you enjoy it and your mind is completely occupied by it. Two hundred scientists were asked if a solution had ever just suddenly occurred to them. Nearly 80 percent said yes—usually when they were taking a break from work.

11 ***3. Trust a hunch based on experience.*** Sometimes a hunch can seem illogical. But if your knowledge and experience tell you the hunch is right, it probably is. One expert said, "I'd seriously consider a solution that came to me in a flash of intuition, even if the facts suggested another answer. Usually my brain has done something very sensible when that happens. It is using previous experience."

12 ***4. Follow up on a hunch.*** A gut feeling works best as a first step in problem solving. That gut feeling often gives a sense that something is right or wrong. But you can't stop there. Many great scientific discoveries began as hunches, but the hunches were always followed by experiments that proved the hunches were right.

13 People faced with a difficult problem or decision are often advised to "use their heads"—that is, to think about it. But experts say that just thinking is not always enough. Psychologist Westcott said, "Purely rational thinking can get you only so far. There comes a time when you have to make the leap and trust your intuition."

BUILDING ACADEMIC VOCABULARY

The words below are on the Academic Word List. Find the words in "When Not to Use Your Head." (The number in parentheses is the number of the paragraph.) If you are not sure what a word means, look it up in your dictionary. Then use the words in the sentences that follow.

apparently (3)	complex (4)	eliminate (5)	statistically (9)
components (4)	acquired (4)	phenomenal (7)	occupy (10)

1. He studied French in school, but he says he acquired most of his knowledge of the language when he lived in Paris.
2. She likes to take a break from work by doing crossword puzzles; she says they ____________________ her mind.
3. A candle was left burning; ____________________ that is how the fire started.
4. She started playing bass guitar with a famous band when she was only 16. Critics agree that she has ____________________ talent.
5. Every year, more people die in car accidents than in plane crashes. So, it is ____________________ safer to fly than to drive.
6. Some doctors say the way to lose weight is to ____________________ high-carbohydrate foods from your diet.
7. The math problem was so ____________________ that even the professor had difficulty explaining it.
8. Scientists have identified all the parts of the substance; they say it has hundreds of chemical ____________________.

DEVELOPING READING SKILLS

UNDERSTANDING THE MAIN IDEAS

There is one correct way to complete each sentence. Circle the letter of the correct answer.

1. Psychologists say that when we use our intuition, we are using
   a. a supernatural ability that only some of us have.
   b. knowledge and experience we carry inside.
   c. a key component of our intelligence.
2. Psychologists say that when we use our intuition, we use it
   a. unconsciously—that is, without even knowing we're using it.
   b. foolishly—that is, when we should be using our rational minds.
   c. consciously—that is, by going through a series of logical steps.

3. Experiments at a university in Canada showed some people could solve problems even though they didn't have all the information they needed. These people
   a. had a sixth sense for making lucky guesses.
   b. were more intelligent than the people who could not solve the problems.
   c. were using knowledge from their own experience.

4. Intuition can help us
   a. understand dreams and predict the future.
   b. solve problems, make discoveries, and make decisions.
   c. forget our problems and be completely relaxed.

READING ACTIVELY

Good readers are active readers; they ask questions and make comments as they read. One way to read actively is to write comments and questions in the margins of the book as you read.

A Look at what one student wrote as he read the first paragraph of "When Not to Use Your Head."

At one time or another, probably everyone has had the feeling that something just wasn't right. Perhaps your body sent you a signal: Your neck muscles tightened, or your stomach went into a knot. Maybe a dream seemed to be warning you of danger. Or maybe you were simply becoming increasingly uncomfortable but couldn't explain why. Probably everyone has had the opposite feeling as well: You just knew that something was right and that everything would turn out fine. Some call these feelings hunches, gut feelings, or a sixth sense. Experts call them intuition.

That's happened to me.

That, too.

How do experts explain intuition?

B Reread "When Not to Use Your Head." As you read, write comments and questions in the margins. Do you think asking questions and making comments can help you be a better reader?

APPLYING INFORMATION

Imagine this: You are in the situations described below. What should you do in each situation? Check the answer an expert on intuition would give. Then explain your choice.

1. You are an experienced cook making soup. You're using a recipe you've never tried before. The recipe tells you to put two teaspoons of salt into the soup. That seems like too much.

   Should you put the two teaspoons of salt into the soup? ☐ Yes ☑ No

   Experts say, "Trust a hunch based on experience."

   As a cook with experience, I can trust my intuition and use less salt.

2. You have always been a little afraid of high bridges. You are about to drive over a high bridge when suddenly you have a strong feeling that something terrible will happen on the bridge.

   Should you drive over the bridge? ☐ Yes ☐ No

3. You are writing an essay as a homework assignment for a class. You seem to be stuck. For the last half hour you've been staring at the paper and haven't written a single word.

   Should you get up and do something else for a while? ☐ Yes ☐ No

4. You are taking a math test. You suddenly have a hunch that the answer to the problem you're working on is "157." You don't know why the answer is "157"; you just know.

   Should you write "157" as your answer and go on to the next problem? ☐ Yes ☐ No

5. Your friend has asked you to color her hair. You have never colored anyone's hair before. The directions on the box of hair color tell you to leave the color on for 20 minutes. You think that can't possibly be enough time.

   Should you leave the color on her hair a little longer? ☐ Yes ☐ No

READING A PIE CHART

Bill Taggart was a university professor and a private consultant who helped people use their intuition. Dr. Taggart believed that intuition comes to us in many forms.

A **Read about the forms that intuition takes, according to Bill Taggart.**

1. Body	a spontaneous movement of the body (Example: You are walking down the street and you suddenly turn left, even though you didn't plan on turning left.)
2. Sensation / Emotion	Sensations: cold shivers, hair standing on end, hands shaking, muscles becoming tight, stomach going into a knot Emotions: joy, sadness, anger, fear (Emotions and sensations often go together—for example, you might feel afraid and then notice your heart is beating fast.)
3. Thought	an idea that suddenly comes to you
4. Image	a visual picture that suddenly appears in your mind

Dr. Taggart asked over 200 students at a university in the United States to describe intuitive experiences that they have had. Then he asked them what form their intuition had taken. Their responses are recorded in the pie chart below. (It is called a "pie chart" because it looks like a pie that is cut into pieces.)

B **Look at the pie chart. Is there anything you find surprising?**

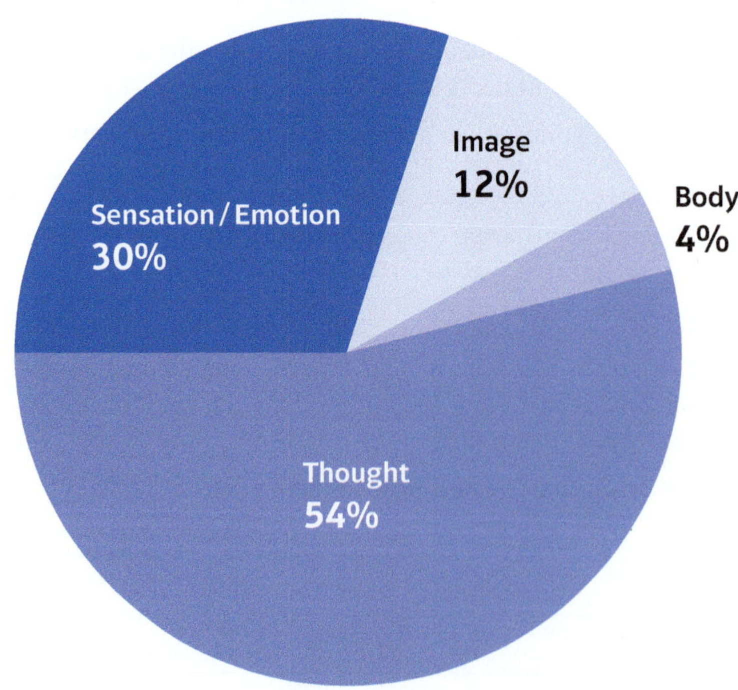

C **Discuss the answers to these questions with your classmates.**

1. What form did intuition take for most of the students?
2. All of the students were studying business. Dr. Taggart thought that fact may explain why so many of them experienced intuition as a thought. Why do you think business students would be more likely to experience intuition as a thought? Do you think art students or music students would be more likely to experience intuition in a different form?
3. Conduct a survey in your class. Ask your classmates what form their intuition usually takes: body, sensation / emotion, thought, or image. Record the results of your survey in a pie chart. Compare the results of your survey with the results of the survey of the business students.
4. Sit with a partner. Ask your partner if he or she has ever had an experience when intuition came in the form of:
   - a spontaneous body movement
   - a sensation or emotion
   - a sudden thought or idea
   - an image

   Ask your partner to tell you more about his or her experience.

DISCUSSION

Psychologists say that when we use our intuition, we are using knowledge and experience that we carry inside us. That knowledge and experience is buried in our subconscious, so we cannot access our intuition whenever we want to use it. Craig Karges, the author of the book *Ignite Your Intuition*, believes people can use a pendulum to access their intuition.

A **Read the steps of the pendulum technique. Then follow the steps alone or in a small group.**

1. Make a pendulum. A pendulum is simply a weight hanging from a string. Your pendulum could be a key ring hanging from a string, or it could be a heavy ring hanging from a piece of thread. The weight needs to be suspended by about six inches (15 centimeters).
2. Draw a chart like the one on the right on a piece of paper.
3. Sit at a table and hold the pendulum by the end of its string. Hold the pendulum with one hand and rest your elbow on the table. Hold the pendulum over the chart, above its center and not quite touching the table.

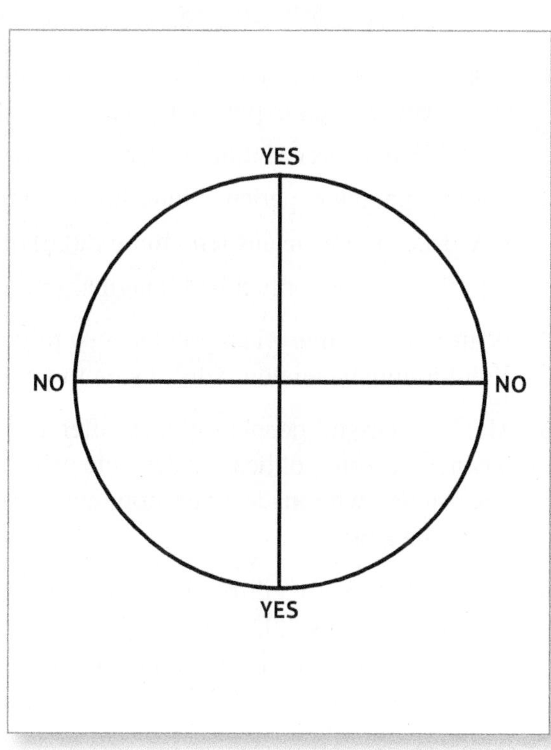

4. Begin by asking a *yes/no* question to which you know the answer, for example, "Is my name ________?" The pendulum should begin to swing slowly back and forth along the *yes* line, perhaps swinging weakly at first and then swinging more strongly. Don't try to get the pendulum to move. Just relax and let it move. Some people will have almost immediate success; others will take longer. Take as much time as you need.

5. Now try asking *yes/no* questions for which you have no sure answer, for example: "Do I need to study more for my math test?" "Should I stay in my present job?" "Is X the right girlfriend for me?" (Most people ask questions about health, finances, and relationships.) If the pendulum swings strongly, you intuitively already knew the answer to your question; you just didn't realize you knew it. If the pendulum swings only weakly or does not swing at all, you probably do not have a strong intuitive answer to your question.

B **Discuss the answers to these questions with your classmates.**

1. Report the results for the pendulum technique. Did the pendulum swing for some people but not for others? Did it swing for people who scored high on the intuition test at the beginning of this unit?
2. Do you think the pendulum technique really helps people get access to their intuition? If so, how does it work? Check the Key on page 131 to see if you guessed correctly.
3. Do you think it is important to use your intuition when making an important decision or solving a difficult problem? Why or why not?
4. Would you consider using this technique to help you make a decision or solve a problem? Why or why not?

WRITING

Choose one of the following topics to write about.

1. Read the following statements about intuition. Is there a statement that you believe to be true because of an experience you have had? Write about your experience.
   - Children are very intuitive, especially around age four or five.
   - Many people experience intuition as something physical.
   - Artists and musicians tend to be intuitive.
   - Intuitive people often had imaginary playmates when they were children.
2. Write about a time when you listened to your intuition and were glad you did. Or write about a time when you didn't listen to your intuition and were sorry you didn't.
3. Many successful people say they often use their intuition. Do you know a story about a businessperson, political leader, scientist, or artist—either a historical figure or someone you know—who made a decision, made a discovery, or solved a problem using intuition? Write the story.
4. People faced with a difficult problem or decision might be told, "Use your head." ("Think carefully.") Or they might be told, "Go with your gut." ("Use your intuition.") Which do you think is better advice: "Use your head" or "Go with your gut"? Explain your answer.

UNIT 6

Neighborhood Feuds

The theme of this unit is neighborhood feuds—arguments between neighbors that often continue for a long time. You will think about problems that people have with their neighbors and how to solve them.

A **What are some things that make neighbors angry? Work in a small group and make a list.**

Example:

1. Loud walking in the apartment upstairs
2. Cooking odors that smell bad

B **Discuss the answers to these questions with your classmates.**

1. Have you had an experience with one of the problems on your list? Tell your classmates about it.
2. Do you have a solution to any of the problems? Tell your classmates your solution.
3. Do you think some of the problems you and your classmates listed are universal—that is, common in every part of the world?

In this unit, you will read about the most famous neighborhood feud in U.S. history. Then you will read about common neighborhood disputes in the United States and how experts recommend resolving them.

A TRUE STORY IN THE NEWS

The Hatfields

Roseanna McCoy

PRE-READING

A **Look at the photos and read the sentences below. The underlined information is not correct. Replace the underlined words with information that is a more logical guess. Write your answers on the lines. Then share your guesses with the class.**

1. Photo 1 was probably taken around 1990. ______________
2. The people in photo 1 were probably all members of the same club. ______________
3. The building behind the people is probably a hospital. ______________
4. They probably lived in a big city. ______________
5. When you look into the eyes of the woman in photo 2, you can see that she was happy. ______________

B **Now read the story on the next page. How many of your guesses were correct?**

Family Feud

1 The most famous family feud in the history of the United States is finally over. The feud between the Hatfield family and the McCoy family, which began in 1878 with an argument over a pig, ended in 2000 with a softball game.

2 In the late 1800s, the Hatfields and the McCoys lived along a river that ran through the Appalachian Mountains, a mountain range in the eastern United States. The Hatfields' log house stood on one side of the river, and the McCoys' stood on the opposite side. The river formed the boundary between Kentucky and West Virginia, so the families lived in different states, even though their houses were less than a mile apart. The large McCoy family, led by 53-year-old Randolph McCoy, had a farm on the Kentucky side of the river. The large Hatfield family, led by 40-year-old William Hatfield, had a farm on the West Virginia side. William Hatfield was known for his hot temper; in fact, his nickname was "Devil." Over the years, he had had arguments with neighbors up and down the river.

3 The trouble between the Hatfields and McCoys began in 1878, when Randolph McCoy accused the Hatfields of stealing one of his pigs. This was a serious charge: On a small farm, one pig could make the difference between having enough meat for the winter and going hungry. The Hatfields denied that they had stolen the pig and refused to return it. McCoy took his case to court, which infuriated William Hatfield. After hearing all the evidence, the jury decided, with a vote of seven to five, that the Hatfields were innocent. McCoy was unhappy about the verdict and grumbled about it, but he accepted it. He did not, however, accept what happened next: His daughter Roseanna fell in love with a Hatfield.

4 Roseanna McCoy met William Hatfield's son Johnse (pronounced John-tsee) at a picnic. She was 21 years old and attractive, with dark eyes and dark hair. He was 18 years old, handsome, and fun-loving. They were instantly attracted to each other and spent the day together. At the end of the day, Johnse told Roseanna he loved her and asked her to marry him. She said yes. That evening, instead of going home to her family, Roseanna went home with Johnse to live with the Hatfield family.

5 The next day, Roseanna and Johnse asked Johnse's father for permission to marry. He refused. No son of his, he said, would ever marry a McCoy. Still, Roseanna stayed with the Hatfields. She thought that once William Hatfield got to know her, once he saw how happy she and Johnse were together, he would change his mind. But weeks went by, and he didn't change his mind.

6 Now Roseanna had no place to go. Knowing that she would never be allowed to marry Johnse, she did not want to continue living with the Hatfields. She could not return to her parents' home because her father was furious with her. Heartbroken, she went to live with an aunt.

7 One day, Roseanna overheard her brothers planning an attack on Johnse. In the middle of the night, she sneaked from her aunt's house and rode on horseback to warn Johnse of the danger. Her warning saved Johnse's life, but still William Hatfield did not permit Roseanna and his son to marry.

8 The next conflict between the Hatfields and the McCoys began—once again—at a picnic. The picnic was held not far from the McCoys' farm, on the Kentucky side of the river, and some Hatfields came across the river to attend. Three of Roseanna McCoy's brothers got into an argument with William Hatfield's brother. The argument turned into a fistfight,

continued ▶

and the McCoys had weapons—a knife and a gun. William Hatfield's brother was stabbed over a dozen times and then shot. Miraculously, he did not die immediately.

9 A local judge took charge. He arrested the three McCoys and ordered some men to take them to jail. The McCoys never arrived at the jail. When William Hatfield heard about his brother, he organized a group of men. The men captured the McCoys and took them across the river, to the Hatfield side. Hatfield told the three McCoys what their fate would be: "If my brother lives," he said, "you'll live. If he dies, you'll die." William Hatfield's brother died the next day. William Hatfield, with the help of relatives, took the three McCoy sons back to the McCoy side of the river and shot them. The Hatfields left the bodies for the McCoy family to find.

10 After the execution of the three McCoy sons, the feud between the Hatfields and the McCoys escalated into a war between the two families. McCoys came across the river and attacked Hatfields; Hatfields came across the river and attacked McCoys. On New Year's Day, 1888, the Hatfields burned the McCoys' home to the ground, killing two of the McCoy children.

11 The burning of the McCoy house caused panic in Kentucky and West Virginia. Rumors flew that whole communities were at war and were burning down towns. The governors of both states assured their citizens that soldiers would restore peace if necessary and sent representatives to investigate the situation. All the representatives came back with the same report: Only two families were fighting.

12 The battle between the Hatfields and the McCoys raged until 1889, when the state of Kentucky brought nine Hatfields to trial for the deaths of the McCoy children. One of the Hatfields was hanged, and the other eight were sentenced to life in prison. After that, the fighting between the two families gradually stopped. By 1890, the war was over. It had lasted 12 years, and 12 people had died.

13 Although the Hatfields and McCoys no longer killed one another, hard feelings between the two families continued for generations. Then, in 2000, a man named Bo McCoy, a descendant of Randolph McCoy, decided it was time to officially end the feud. He announced that there would be a reunion of the McCoys and Hatfields in a small town in Kentucky. Over 1,100 people—all descendants of William Hatfield and Randolph McCoy—came to the reunion. For three days, Hatfields and McCoys mingled. They ate together, listened to music, and swapped stories that their grandparents and great-grandparents had told them about the feud.

14 The weekend reunion ended with a friendly game of softball, the Hatfields against the McCoys. Shouting and cheering, Hatfields and McCoys sat side by side and watched as nine members of the Hatfield family played against nine members of the McCoy family. The McCoys won the softball game, 14 to 1. The Hatfields were good-natured about their defeat, and not one Hatfield ran to get his shotgun. The feud was over.

GETTING THE BIG PICTURE

The Hatfield-McCoy feud lasted 12 years and left 12 people dead. What is the main reason the feud became so serious and lasted so long? Circle the letter of your answer.

a. The Hatfields wanted the McCoys' land and animals and would not stop fighting until they had them.

b. The governors of Kentucky and West Virginia could not stop the fighting because whole communities were at war.

c. The problems between the Hatfields and the McCoys escalated; that is, each problem led to a bigger problem.

BUILDING VOCABULARY

RECALLING NEW WORDS

The words below are from the story. Complete each sentence with the correct word.

accused	escalated	refused	verdict
assured	fate	rumors	weapons
denied	mingled	softball	

1. Randolph McCoy said he believed that the Hatfields had taken one of his pigs. He ____accused____ the Hatfield family of stealing.

2. William Hatfield said it was not true that his family had taken the pig. He ________________ stealing it.

3. After listening to both sides of the story, the jury made an official decision: Their ________________ was that the Hatfields were innocent.

4. When Johnse and Roseanna asked William Hatfield if they could marry, he said that no son of his would ever marry a McCoy. He ________________ to give his son permission.

5. The McCoy sons had two ________________—a knife and a gun.

6. William Hatfield told the McCoy sons what would happen if his brother died: Their ________________ would be the same as his brother's.

7. After the deaths of William Hatfield's brother and the McCoy sons, the fighting between the Hatfields and the McCoys got much worse. It ________________ into a war between the two families.

8. One person told another person about the burning of the McCoy house, and then that person told another. Before long, ________________ were spreading that entire towns were being burned.

9. The governors told people not to worry: It was not true that whole communities were at war. They ________________ people that peace would be restored.

10. At the reunion, Hatfields and McCoys met and talked with each other. They ____________________ for three days.

11. The Hatfields and McCoys wanted to be sure that nobody got hurt playing baseball at their reunion. So they played ____________________, a type of baseball that is a little safer.

RECOGNIZING RELATED WORDS

"Family Feud" is about a problem between two families. Nine words in the story are related to the word *problem*. In the list below, find the nine words that are related to *problem*. Circle them. The first one is done for you.

history	governor	war	nickname
argument	conflict	battle	fistfight
hard feelings	trouble	reunion	feud
picnic	report	fighting	

DEVELOPING READING SKILLS

ORGANIZING INFORMATION BY DRAWING A PICTURE

Historical accounts—like the story of the Hatfields and McCoys—can be difficult to understand because there are many names of people and places. Sometimes it helps to draw a picture as you read. The picture not only helps you understand the story; it also helps you remember it.

The picture below organizes the information in paragraphs 2 and 4 of "Family Feud." The names of some people and places are missing from the picture. Write each name on the correct line.

Johnse	West Virginia	Randolph McCoy	Appalachian

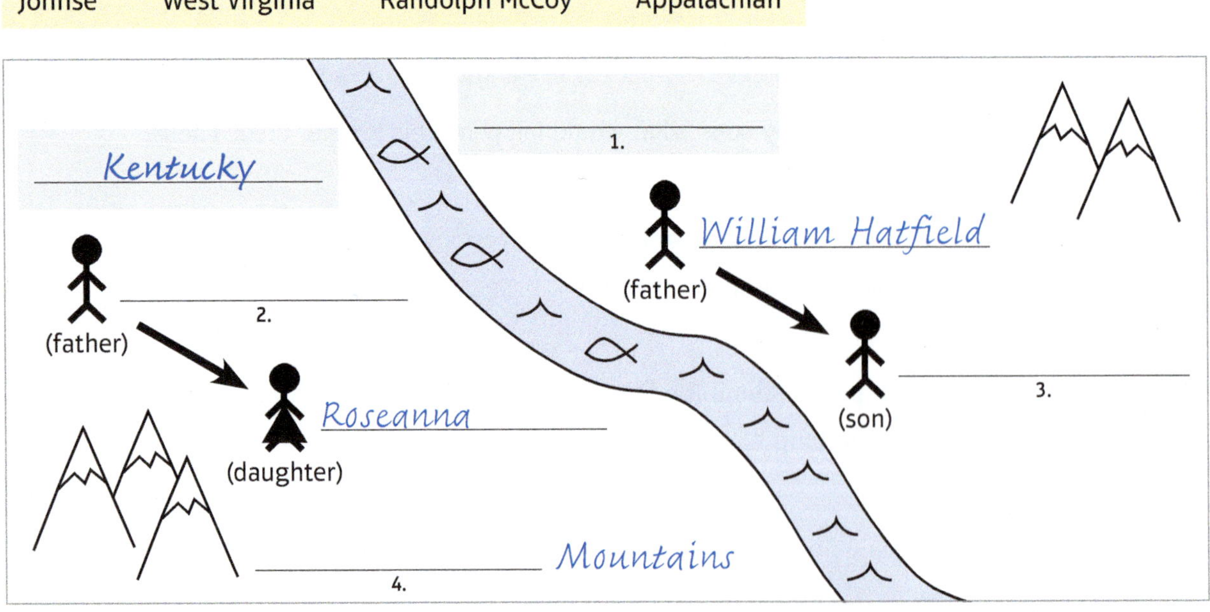

ORGANIZING INFORMATION BY MAKING A TIME LINE

Another way to organize the information in a historical account is to make a *time line*—a list of events in the order in which they happened. A time line can help you understand the events in a story more clearly.

Below is a time line of the events in "Family Feud." The following sentences are missing from the time line. Complete the time line by writing each sentence in the correct place.

- Randolph McCoy's sons get into an argument with William Hatfield's brother, who is stabbed and shot.
- The Hatfields burn the McCoys' house down, killing two McCoy children.
- Roseanna McCoy and Johnse Hatfield fall in love. William Hatfield does not permit their marriage.
- The Hatfield-McCoy war is over. Twelve people are dead.

Hatfield-McCoy Feud Time Line

1878	1. Randolph McCoy accuses the Hatfields of stealing his pig; a jury decides that the Hatfields are innocent.
	2. ______________________
	3. Roseanna overhears her brothers' plans to attack Johnse and warns him, saving his life.
	4. ______________________
	5. William Hatfield captures the McCoy sons and kills them after his brother dies.
1888	6. ______________________
1889	7. Kentucky brings nine Hatfields to trial for the deaths of the McCoy children. One Hatfield is hanged; eight are sentenced to life in prison.
1890	8. ______________________
2000	9. Over 1,100 descendants of Randolph McCoy and William Hatfield hold a friendly reunion in Kentucky.

UNDERSTANDING CAUSE AND EFFECT

Complete each sentence. Write your answer on the lines. (There may be several correct ways to complete each sentence.)

1. The Hatfields and the McCoys lived along the same river, but in separate states because the river formed the boundary between two states.

2. William Hatfield's nickname was "Devil" because ______________________________.

3. Randolph McCoy took the Hatfields to court because ______________________________.

4. Roseanna McCoy didn't want to continue living with the Hatfields because ______________________________.

5. In the middle of the night, Roseanna sneaked out of her aunt's house because ______________________________.

6. William Hatfield killed the three McCoy sons because ______________________________.

7. The governors of West Virginia and Kentucky sent representatives to investigate the conflict between the Hatfields and the McCoys because ______________________________.

8. The state of Kentucky brought nine Hatfields to trial because ______________________________.

9. In 2000, a descendant of Randolph McCoy announced a reunion of the Hatfields and the McCoys because ______________________________.

NEWS AND VIEWS

When he thought the Hatfields had stolen one of his pigs, Randolph McCoy tried to resolve the conflict by going to court. What is the best way to resolve conflicts between neighbors? The author of the following article has some suggestions.

A **Preview the article before you read it—that is, read short parts before you read the whole text. Preview this way:**

1. Read the title and subheadings.
2. Read the first paragraph.
3. Read the first sentence of every paragraph.
4. Read the last paragraph.

B **Now read the article. As you read, think about this: Did previewing the article make it easier for you to understand it?**

Neighborhood Feuds by Mark Stuart Gill

1 Across the United States, disputes between neighbors are becoming common. The most common conflicts fall into three categories: excessive noise; damage caused by children and pets; and trees (for instance, a neighbor's maple tree blocking your view).

2 As trivial as these irritations may seem, when they occur repeatedly they can start all-out war. For instance, in one California town, a man was so enraged by persistent barking from his neighbor's dog that he taped the pet's mouth shut. The dog died, and the man now faces criminal charges for animal cruelty. In a Connecticut neighborhood, when a family refused to trim their messy weeping-willow tree, someone drilled holes in the tree's trunk and poisoned it.

3 When a neighbor problem arises, people usually try to avoid the neighbor. They are afraid they will insult or offend the neighbor if they talk about the problem. That is probably not the best tactic; avoiding a problem neighbor makes people feel helpless, like there is no solution.

4 Lawsuits are also usually a poor solution. A lawyer who specializes in neighbor problems says, "Courts hate neighbor lawsuits. Lawsuits often just mask the real problems between neighbors. So, even after the lawsuit is over, the neighbors find something else to fight about."

What You Can Do

5 So, if avoiding a problem neighbor isn't an effective solution, and neither is filing a lawsuit, how do you handle a dispute with a neighbor? Experts say to handle it yourself.

6 To begin with, know your rights. When a neighbor does something extremely unreasonable, he or she has probably broken a "nuisance law." These laws vary from community to community, but they are often very detailed. For instance in Farmington, New Mexico, music played on private property is not allowed to exceed fifty decibels at night. Check the local laws at your town clerk's office or the public library. If you have legal grounds to complain, show your neighbor a copy of the law.

7 Unfortunately, being on the right side of the law isn't always enough. To prevent the

continued ▶

problem from turning into a battle, keep in mind that different types of neighbor problems call for different strategies:

8 ***Noise.*** Experts in neighborhood mediation advise people to remember that noise is subjective. The neighbor might not even realize he or she is creating a problem. You might think that the rock 'n' roll band next door is making noise, but they think they are making important music. When you approach a neighbor about a noise problem, don't criticize the neighbor's behavior; that might only make the neighbor angry. Instead, tell your neighbor how the sound is affecting you. For example, instead of saying, "Your guitars are too loud," say, "Your guitars are keeping me and my family awake at night."

9 ***Kids and pets.*** Children and domestic animals have the greatest potential to tear a neighborhood apart. Take the case of Michael Rubin, who was involved in one of the most bitter neighbor lawsuits in the United States.

10 One day Rubin came home and decided to take a nap. Outside his bedroom window, the boy next door was playing basketball. Rubin recalls, "I asked the boy to stop playing basketball. He stopped, but then came out with his father and started playing again." Rubin grabbed a garden hose and soaked the boy and his father.

11 The neighbors sued Rubin. They claimed that his spraying them with water caused such emotional distress, they had to go into therapy, and they wanted him to pay for it. Rubin countersued his neighbors.

12 What can neighbors do to avoid this legal and emotional war? In a case involving a neighbor's child, it pays to be especially careful. People can be hypersensitive and defensive about their kids. Instead of reacting in the heat of the moment, take some time to think about how you want to solve the problem. Then calmly approach your neighbors.

13 ***Trees.*** Trees are one of the trickiest neighbor problems to resolve. That's because they serve so many vital purposes to a homeowner. They may be used for privacy, shade, fences, property line markers, or even food. So, in the case of a problem tree, be prepared to compromise.

14 That's something Amy King wishes she had done. Every autumn, Amy collected the apples that dropped from her neighbor's trees into her yard, to make cider. There was no fence between the yards, so Amy collected only the apples that she was sure had fallen on her side of the property line. Last year, her neighbor gave her a bill. "The trees belong to me," he said. "If you want to use my apples, you have to pay for them."

15 Furious, Amy trimmed the apple-tree branches that hung over her property line. The neighbor fought back: He hired a tree consultant who claimed the trees were traumatized, and he wanted payment for the damage.

16 She could have avoided these troubles by compromising with her neighbor. For instance, she might have suggested that she'd be willing to allow the branches to hang over her property—and not collect the apples—if her neighbor would remove the apples that fell into her yard.

Declaring a Truce

17 Unfortunately, some neighbors are not willing to be reasonable. Instead, they become threatening, even violent.

18 In such cases, the ideal solution may be to bring in a neutral third party to mediate. Neighbor mediation is remarkably successful. The American Bar Association reports that, on average, over 250,000 neighbors a year try mediation to resolve disputes. Of those, 80 percent reach a satisfactory written agreement.

19 In short, if you are having a dispute with your neighbor, don't avoid the neighbor and don't file a lawsuit. It is unlikely that either of those tactics will work. Try handling the problem yourself, remembering to use these strategies: Don't criticize your neighbor's behavior; instead, explain how the behavior is affecting you. Rather than react in the heat of the moment, think about what you want to say and then say it calmly. Be ready to compromise. If your neighbors are breaking the law, show them a copy of the law. If these strategies don't work, try mediation—a tactic that will work almost 80 percent of the time.

BUILDING VOCABULARY

UNDERSTANDING ACADEMIC VOCABULARY

The words below are on the Academic Word List. Find the words in "Neighborhood Feuds." (The number in parentheses is the number of the paragraph.) If you are not sure what a word means, look it up in your dictionary. Then use the words in the sentences that follow.

categories (1)	exceeding (6)	potential (9)	resolve (13)
persistent (2)	strategy (7)	involved in (9)	neutral (18)
vary (6)	domestic (9)		

1. She has a ten-page paper due in three weeks. She plans to do research the first week, write an outline and rough draft the second week, and type the final draft the third week. That's her ____strategy____ for getting the paper finished on time.
2. Switzerland refuses to take sides in international conflicts and for centuries has remained ____________ in wartime.
3. He always seems to be unhappy with the grades he gets; right now, he is ____________ a dispute with his English professor over the grade he got on his essay.
4. The tickets ____________ in price: Seats near the stage cost \$50, but balcony seats cost only \$15.
5. Businesses are complaining that cooking odors from a neighborhood restaurant are coming into their shops. The restaurant hopes to ____________ the dispute, perhaps by installing a large fan.
6. Doctors are warning people that some weight-loss pills can possibly cause health problems; some pills even have the ____________ for causing heart attacks.
7. She was driving 70 miles per hour in a 55-mile-per-hour zone. She got a ticket for ____________ the speed limit.
8. She's been coughing since she caught a cold a month ago. Today she's going to the doctor for medicine for her ____________ cough.
9. Police officers are careful when trying to resolve a conflict between a husband and wife in their home; ____________ arguments can sometimes become violent.
10. Parking spaces at the university fall into three ____________: parking for visitors; parking for staff and faculty; and parking for students who commute from home to campus.

UNDERSTANDING LEGAL TERMS

Imagine this: You are having a problem with a neighbor. Read the description of the problem. Then match each boldfaced legal term used in the description with a meaning in the list below. Write the letter of your answer on the line.

Description of the problem

Your neighbor Joe has piles of trash in his yard. You've asked him to remove the trash and he has refused. Joe says there's nothing you can do about the piles of trash. He says you have no legal (a) ***grounds*** to complain. But you know (b) ***your rights***. You decide to (c) ***file a lawsuit***. You claim in your lawsuit that your house has lost value because of Joe's trash and you want him to remove the trash.

When Joe learns that you have filed a lawsuit against him, he is upset. He says he is so upset that he can't eat or sleep. He (d) ***countersues***: He wants you to pay him money for upsetting him. You try to resolve your dispute with Joe by asking a (e) ***third party*** to help you and Joe talk about your problem. But Joe does not agree to the mediation.

In the middle of the night you go into Joe's yard and take the trash. When Joe sees that his trash is gone, he calls the police. You admit to the police that you are the one who took the trash. Now the police say you (f) ***face criminal charges***!

Meanings of legal terms

__d__ 1. responds to your lawsuit against him by suing you

_____ 2. might be guilty of a crime, and you will have to go through a legal process

_____ 3. go to court and officially record your complaint against Joe

_____ 4. neutral person—someone who is not a friend of either you or Joe

_____ 5. what you are allowed to do

_____ 6. reasons

DEVELOPING READING SKILLS

UNDERSTANDING THE MAIN IDEAS

Use the phrases and words below to complete sentences 1–4. Write your answers on the lines.

explain to your neighbor how the behavior is affecting you
bring in a neutral third party to mediate
~~avoid the neighbor~~
check to see if your neighbor has broken a law
take some time to cool off; then calmly approach your neighbor
file a lawsuit
compromise

1. If you have a problem with a neighbor, you should not
   a. avoid the neighbor.
   b. __________.
2. If a neighbor does something extremely unreasonable, the first thing you should do is __________.
3. Three strategies that usually work for solving neighbor problems are
   a. __________.
   b. __________.
   c. __________.
4. If the three strategies above do not work, and your neighbor becomes threatening or violent, then the ideal solution may be to __________.

APPLYING INFORMATION

Do the following activities with your classmates.

1. Read the list of neighbor problems you and your classmates made at the beginning of this unit on page 85. If you would like to add problems to the list, do so. Think about the strategies for resolving neighbor disputes suggested in the article "Neighborhood Feuds," as well as the solutions you and your classmates suggested at the beginning of this unit.
2. With a partner, choose one of the problems on the list. Then role-play with your partner. One person plays the part of the neighbor causing the problem, and the other person plays the part of the neighbor trying to find a solution. (A third classmate can be a mediator—a neutral third party who tries to help you resolve your dispute.)
3. Role-play your conversation with your "neighbor" in front of the class.

READING A LIST

A Shelley Whalen, a mediator who helps settle disputes in Ohio, made a list of the top causes of neighborhood feuds there. The most common problems are at the top of the list and the least common problems are at the bottom. Read the list.

Top Seven Causes of Neighborhood Feuds in Ohio, U.S.A.

1. **Noise**
   dogs barking, loud music, noisy children
2. **Control of pets**
   pets coming into neighbor's yard
3. **Condition of yard**
   lawn not mowed, litter, hedges not trimmed
4. **Control of children**
   children coming into neighbor's yard
5. **Parking**
   neighbors and their guests parking in front of others' homes
6. **Trees and hedges**
   tree hanging over neighbor's roof; tree blocking view; tree creating a mess; hedge blocking visibility, making it dangerous for neighbor to pull out of driveway
7. **Rumors and gossip**
   people spreading rumors that neighbors are getting divorced, are in financial trouble, can't control their children, etc.

Rumors and gossip are sometimes the real reasons behind complaints 1–6.

B Make a list of problems that cause conflicts between neighbors in your country. Give an example of each problem.

Example:

1. Trash (leaving trash in the hallway)
2. Noise (loud parties late at night)

C Compare your list with the list made by a classmate from a different country. Are there any problems that are common in your partner's country but not in yours?

DISCUSSION

A **Below are descriptions of actual neighborhood feuds. Read about the feuds. Then, in a small group, decide on a fair way to resolve each dispute. Tell the group how the dispute would be resolved in your country.**

1. A man in southern Germany likes to grill bratwurst (sausages that are popular in Germany) in his yard. His neighbor doesn't like the smoke.

2. A church in Washington, D.C., has a large kitchen and wants to give free meals to the poor and homeless. Neighbors do not want the "soup kitchen" to open. They are worried that the people coming for free meals will bring more crime into the area.

3. A California woman has piles of trash in her yard. She has three old cars, a rusted washer and dryer, several bookcases, a sofa, old tires, shopping carts, an old table and chairs, and chunks of concrete in front of her house. The neighbors are tired of looking at the junk, and the houses nearest the woman's house have lost value.

4. A billionaire in the state of Washington is building a "monster house"—a house ten times bigger than the other houses in the neighborhood. The mansion will be under construction for two years. Neighbors are complaining that building the house has turned their neighborhood into a construction zone, with dump trucks, bulldozers, and work crews arriving at 6 a.m. One neighbor is suing the billionaire for $1 million. "The noise is unbearable," she says.

5. A parrot named Bubba is causing trouble in a Florida neighborhood. His owner keeps the parrot on her screened-in balcony. Neighbors claim the parrot's loud screeches bother them. They also claim that the parrot uses bad words. One neighbor says the parrot told her, "Shut up, you #%@*&!" Bubba's owner says the parrot is learning the bad words not from her, but from the neighbors. She refuses to bring the parrot inside.

B **Share your group's ideas for resolving the disputes with the class. Then check the** **Key on page 131** **to see how the disputes were actually resolved.**

WRITING

Choose one of the following topics to write about.

1. Describe a neighbor that you have or once had.
2. Have you ever had a dispute with a neighbor? What was the dispute about? How was the dispute resolved?
3. Roseanna McCoy was not allowed to marry Johnse Hatfield because their fathers hated one another. Do you have a story in your own family about someone who was not permitted to marry the person he or she loved?
4. A line in a poem by Robert Frost is "Good fences make good neighbors." What do you think the line means? Do you think it is true?
5. The author of "Neighborhood Feuds" gives these suggestions for resolving conflicts between neighbors:
   - Don't criticize your neighbor's behavior; instead, explain how the behavior is affecting you.
   - Rather than react in the heat of the moment, think about what you want to say and then say it calmly.
   - Be ready to compromise.

   These strategies seem to work in the United States. Would they work just as well in your country? Explain why they would or wouldn't.

UNIT 7

The Stock Market

In this unit, you will read about the stock market. A stock is a part of a company that people can buy. The "stock market" refers to the value of stocks and the business of buying and selling them.

A **Look at the photo. Answer the questions.**

1. What is the person doing?
2. Is there good news or bad news on the screen?
3. What do you think the person will do next?

B **Which of the words below do you think you will probably find in this unit? Circle them.**

company	investor	pizza	stockbroker
health	library	product	stockholder
investment strategy	money manager	profit	stock portfolio

In this unit, you will read about a woman who made a lot of money—$22 million, to be exact. Then you will read about a group of women who followed some simple rules for investing in the stock market. Did the women make money? Read their story to find out.

A TRUE STORY IN THE NEWS

PRE-READING

Look at the photo and read the title of the story on the next page. Then think about these questions. Discuss your answers with your classmates.

1. What do you think the statue of the bull represents? What do you think the statue of the girl represents? (They are works of art, so they can mean different things to different people. Check the Key on page 131 to see some possible answers.)
2. The woman in the next story, Anne Scheiber, invested her small savings in the stock market and made a fortune. Do you think she was particularly smart? Or particularly lucky?
3. Do you think anyone can do what Anne Scheiber did?

A Smart Investor

1 While Anne Scheiber was alive, no one paid much attention to her. She had no husband, no friends, and hardly any contact with her four brothers and four sisters. She rarely left her small apartment, and when she did go out, she was almost invisible—a short, thin woman dressed entirely in black. But when she died at age 101, Anne Scheiber suddenly became famous. It turned out that Miss Scheiber was rich, and she left her fortune—$22 million—to Yeshiva University in New York City, a school she had never attended and never even visited.

2 The story of how Anne Scheiber made her fortune is as fascinating as why she gave it all away. Anne's father died when she was a child, leaving her mother with nine children to support. Anne's mother managed to feed and clothe her family, but money was tight. Whenever the family had any extra money, it went to educate the four sons; the five daughters were on their own.

3 Anne started working as a bookkeeper when she was 15 and went to school at night, eventually graduating from college with a law degree. She decided not to practice law, however. Instead, she went to work for the Internal Revenue Service (the I.R.S.) in Washington, D.C., as a tax auditor. Her job was to examine income tax returns and look for errors. Anne was a diligent employee who excelled at her work. Although she was only five feet tall and weighed 100 pounds, her favorite technique was to scare people when she thought they were cheating on their taxes. "These are not the correct figures," she would tell them. "Come back tomorrow with the real figures." She was described as "a terror." Yet, in the 23 years that Anne worked for the I.R.S., she was never promoted, and she got only small pay raises.

4 Anne learned two lessons in her years of working at the I.R.S. First, she concluded that women had little chance of succeeding, no matter how hard they worked. Second, from examining thousands of income tax records she learned that the surest way to get rich in the United States was to invest in stocks. Anne Scheiber felt that the I.R.S. had treated her unfairly, and she wanted revenge. She decided to get even by getting rich. Even though she was earning very little money, she saved as much as she could; some years, she saved 80 percent of her salary. Then she used her savings to invest in the stock market. By 1936, she had $21,000 invested in stocks. But it wasn't until 1944, when Anne retired at age 50, that she became a full-time investor.

5 Anne retired from the I.R.S. with a small pension and a savings account of $5,000 in cash. She moved to New York City, the financial center of the United States, and rented a small apartment. Then she began to study the stock market in the same diligent way she had studied income tax returns. She decided to invest first in industries she knew something about. She loved Hollywood movies, so she investigated the studios. Which studios were the most successful? Using information she got from newspapers at the public library, she kept track of attendance records for recent movies. Two studios—Paramount and Universal—seemed to produce the most popular movies. She bought stock in both studios. She bought stock in a broadcasting company called Capital Cities, which later became Disney Corporation. She bought stock in Coca-Cola and later in Pepsi-Cola. She bought stock in drug companies like Bristol-Myers Squibb and Schering-Plough.

6 Anne's investment strategy was simple. First, she didn't put all her eggs in one basket—she ultimately invested in 100 companies, not just in one or two. Second, she invested only in leading companies whose products she understood. Third, she almost never sold stocks. When the value of her stocks fell, she hung on to them, convinced they would be worth something in the long run.

7 By 1970, Anne Scheiber had turned her small savings into a stock portfolio worth millions, but she certainly didn't live like a millionaire. Her home was the same tiny apartment she rented when she moved to New York, furnished with the same tables, chairs, and lamps she

continued ▶

had bought in 1944. Paint was peeling off the walls, and dust covered the bookcases. She often skipped meals to save money on food, and she walked everywhere to save money on bus fare, even when it rained. She never bought a newspaper—instead, she walked to the library and read the *Wall Street Journal* there—and she rarely bought new clothes. Everywhere she went, she wore the same cheap black coat—fall, winter, and spring. (Once, a niece bought her a new black coat, and when Anne found out that it had cost $150, she refused to wear it.) Saving and investing money was her obsession. Every penny Anne had, she used to buy stocks.

8 The sacrifices Anne made to invest in the stock market were not only material; there were social sacrifices, too. Her entire world was her investments. She shut out her family and friends, and she never had a sweetheart. The only social events Anne attended were stockholders' meetings of the companies whose stock she owned. Whenever a stockholders' meeting was in New York City, Anne Scheiber was there. She would go directly to the CEO of the company and demand answers to her questions, just as she had when she was an auditor at the I.R.S. In the last years of her life, Anne left her apartment only to visit her lawyer, her stockbroker, or to see her stock certificates, which were kept in a vault in her stockbroker's offices near Wall Street. She would walk to the offices, look over her stock certificates, and then walk back to her apartment. "She did that a lot," her stockbroker says.

9 When Anne Scheiber died in 1995 at the age of 101, she had $22 million in stocks. In her will, she left $50,000 to the niece who had bought her the black coat, and she gave the rest of the money to Yeshiva University. She specified that the money was to be used for scholarships and loans for women only. In the end, Anne Scheiber did indeed get even: There is no tax on money given to schools, so not one penny of Anne's fortune went to her former employer, the I.R.S.

10 When news of Anne Scheiber's $22 million gift spread, she suddenly got the attention she had never had while she was alive. People poured over her stock portfolio, curious to see which stocks had made her a multimillionaire. Newspapers called her "amazing," "wise," and "brilliant." But money managers pointed out that one didn't have to be a genius to accomplish what Anne Scheiber did. Anne Scheiber began buying stocks as early as 1936 and died in 1995. So, she owned some stocks for over 50 years. According to money managers, that investment strategy—buying stock and holding onto it for a long time—has always been successful. Yes, they said, Anne Scheiber was smart. But perhaps the smartest thing she did was live to be 101.

GETTING THE BIG PICTURE

What were the reasons for Anne Scheiber's success in the stock market? Check (✓) two reasons.

☐ 1. When her father died, she received a small fortune and invested it in the stock market.

☐ 2. She used wise investment strategies: investing in more than one company, investing only in leading companies, and not selling stocks.

☐ 3. Friends who were the CEOs of big companies told her which stocks to buy.

☐ 4. She owned some stocks for over 50 years.

BUILDING VOCABULARY

RECALLING NEW WORDS

Read each sentence. What is the meaning of the word(s) in *italics*? Circle the letter of the correct answer.

1. Anne Scheiber saw her family only once or twice a year. She had *hardly any* contact with them.
   (a.) almost no
   b. regular

2. After she died, Anne Scheiber got the attention she never had while she was alive. People found her story *fascinating*.
   a. very interesting
   b. difficult to believe

3. The Scheiber family never went on vacations, never ate at restaurants, and never owned a new car. *Money was tight.*
   a. There was not enough money.
   b. All their money was in the bank.

4. Anne worked during the day and went to classes only at night, so it took her years to finish school. *Eventually*, she graduated from college with a degree in law.
   a. after a lot of hard work
   b. after a long time

5. If Anne thought people were not being honest, she would say, "These are not the correct figures. Come back tomorrow with the real figures!" Her *technique* usually worked.
   a. way of doing something
   b. angry words

6. In the 23 years that Anne worked at the I.R.S., she always had the same job. She was never *promoted*.
   a. told she was doing a good job
   b. given a more important, higher-paying job

7. Anne believed that the I.R.S. had been unfair to her. She wanted to *get even*.
   a. hurt the I.R.S. as much as the I.R.S. had hurt her
   b. ask the I.R.S. for a big pay raise and a promotion

8. Anne didn't worry when the price of her stocks fell because she believed that they would make money in the future. She was sure they would be worth something *in the long run*.
   a. if she sold them
   b. at a later time
9. Anne never bought new clothes, new furniture, or even a newspaper. She *made a lot of sacrifices* to save money.
   a. had the help of many people
   b. gave up many things she wanted or needed
10. Anne could think of nothing else but saving and investing money. It was her *obsession*.
    a. an extreme, unhealthy interest in something
    b. something you do in your free time because you find it enjoyable
11. At stockholders' meetings, Anne would ask the *CEO* questions about the company.
    a. the chief executive officer, the person with the most authority in a company
    b. the company export official, the person in charge of sales to foreign countries
12. When Anne wrote her will, she knew exactly whom she wanted to get her money. She *specified* that the money was for female students only.
    a. hoped it would be possible
    b. stated in an exact and detailed way

USING NEW WORDS

A Complete the sentences with examples from your own life.

1. I have hardly any ____.
2. I think it's fascinating to learn about ____.
3. When money is tight, I don't ____.
4. Eventually, I hope to ____.
5. I know a good technique for ____.
6. I would try to get even if someone ____.
7. I would make sacrifices in order to ____.
8. If I wrote my will, I would specify that ____.

B In small groups, take turns reading your sentences aloud. Ask your classmates questions about their sentences.

DEVELOPING READING SKILLS

UNDERSTANDING CAUSE AND EFFECT

Complete the sentences. Write your answer on the line. The first one is done for you.

1. When Anne Scheiber died, she suddenly became famous because *she gave her fortune of $22 million to a university*.
2. Money was always tight for the Scheiber family because ______________________.
3. Anne wanted to get even with her employer, the I.R.S., because ______________________.
4. Anne decided to invest her money in the stock market because ______________________.
5. Anne never bought new furniture, clothes, or even a newspaper because ______________________.
6. No male students at Yeshiva University received any money from Anne Scheiber because ______________________.
7. Yeshiva University didn't pay tax on the $22 million they received from Anne Scheiber because ______________________.
8. Money managers said that Anne Scheiber made a fortune in the stock market mainly because ______________________.

UNDERSTANDING MAIN IDEAS AND SUPPORTING DETAILS

The ability to understand the main ideas and the details that support them is an important reading skill.

Main ideas are important facts and events; without them, a story doesn't make sense. *Supporting details* often make a story more interesting, but the story would still make sense without them. For example, the fact that Anne Scheiber had a law degree is not a main idea of the story; the story would still make sense without that information.

Check (✓) the six facts that give you the main ideas of Anne Scheiber's story.

Anne Scheiber

- [ ] 1. had four sisters and four brothers.
- [ ] 2. dressed entirely in black.
- [x] 3. worked for the I.R.S as a tax auditor.
- [ ] 4. was five feet tall and weighed 100 pounds.

- ☐ 5. believed that the I.R.S. was unfair to her.
- ☐ 6. wanted to get even with the I.R.S. by getting rich.
- ☐ 7. loved Hollywood movies.
- ☐ 8. made great sacrifices so that she could invest every penny she had in the stock market.
- ☐ 9. read the *Wall Street Journal* at the library.
- ☐ 10. often walked to her stockbroker's offices to look at her stock certificates.
- ☐ 11. had a fortune of $22 million when she died.
- ☐ 12. gave almost all her money to a university, specifying it was for women only.

EXPANDING ON THE STORY

Imagine this: After Anne Scheiber died, a newspaper reporter interviewed people who knew her. Role-play the interviews. One student plays the role of the reporter. The other students play the parts of the people below. Conduct the interviews "live" in class. The reporter's questions are given, and the first answer is done for you.

Reporter: Did you know Anne Scheiber well?

Neighbor: *I hardly ever saw her. She stayed in her apartment most of the time and didn't socialize with the neighbors. I'd see her come and go once in a while, but I never talked to her.*

Reporter: I understand that you once gave your aunt a gift that she returned. Could you tell us about that?

Niece: ______________________

Reporter: Is it true that Anne Scheiber attended stockholders' meetings? What did she do there?

CEO: ______________________

Reporter: What kind of worker was Anne Scheiber? Do you think she was happy at the I.R.S.?

I.R.S. co-worker: ______________________

Reporter: Could you briefly describe Ms. Scheiber's investment strategies?

Anne's stockbroker: ______________________

NEWS AND VIEWS

Anne Scheiber made millions by investing in the stock market. But not everyone is successful when they invest. Some people actually lose money. Are there rules to follow when you invest in the stock market—rules that make it more likely that you will make money? The women in the next story believed there were rules, and they followed those rules carefully. Did they make money?

Read the article, and you will find out.

How to Build a Nest Egg

1 Karin Housely, a wife and mother of four young children, was worried about her family's financial future. Her husband earned a good salary, yet they never saved any money. How would they pay for their children's college educations? Would they have enough money in their retirement years? What would happen if her husband got sick or injured and couldn't work?

2 Karin learned that many of her friends had the same problem. Not one of their families had a "nest egg"—money saved for the future. So, Karin invited nine friends to form an investment club. First, the women learned all they could about saving and investing money. They concluded that the best way to invest money was to buy stocks in some good companies. They agreed that they would each contribute $50 every month and put their money together to buy stocks. They also agreed that they would not sell their stock for a long time—they would buy and hold. Then, years later, they would all have nest eggs.

3 Although the women knew they wanted to invest in "good" companies, they weren't sure how to determine which companies were good. So they did more research. They decided on twelve investment strategies they would use when buying stocks. Here are four of their investment strategies, explained by the women in their own words.

continued ▶

1. Buy What You Know

by Cheryl

4 "Buy what you know" is my favorite tip. It's the only one of our principles that requires no research other than simply paying attention to your own life. Yipee! That I can do! Immediately, we are all transformed into expert stockpickers. "What?" you say. "Me? An expert? Already?" That's right. Open your refrigerator: What brand of ketchup do you buy? Soft drinks? Orange juice? Look in your pocket or purse: Which company made your smartphone? Go to the Internet: What is your favorite Web site? Start by looking at companies that are familiar to you—ones you know and love—and buy what you know.

5 Since this is the first step, I want to make sure you realize that buying what you know doesn't mean buying *everything* you know. This is simply the technique we use to get our list of stocks we will research.

2. K.I.S.S. (Keep It Super Simple)

by Cheryl

6 If you are thinking about buying stock in a company, be sure you understand exactly what the company does. Peter Lynch (one of the most famous and successful investors) says you should be able to explain what a company does to a 10-year-old child and draw its product with a crayon. When you understand a company and its industry, you can more easily predict whether its product or service is going to be in demand in the coming years.

3. Leader in Its Field

by Megan

7 Is the company the leader in its field? Would everyone recognize the name if you said it? To look for the top brands in an industry, name the first company that comes to your mind when you say, for example, "chocolate" or "fast-food restaurant" or "computer." These companies are all top dogs, leaders in their field. When you look for companies, look for the top dog. We don't want to invest in small start-up companies. They're too risky. We want the leaders in the field because they are established and proven.

4. Repeat Profitability

by Karin

8 How many times do you pick up your phone each day? How many times do you turn on the lights? How many trips do you make to the gas station every month? How many soft drinks do you drink each week?

9 Repeaters are companies that have products that the consumer purchases often. For instance, I am addicted to Diet Coke. I have to have one Diet Coke a day...at noon. The Coca-Cola company must love me. Day in, day out, they can count on me coming back. Another example of a Repeater would be a pharmaceutical company. Just think of the millions of people who need to take some form of medication each day. I look at my Dad's medicine cabinet, and I think he single-handedly keeps the pharmaceutical companies in business.

10 Why invest in a Repeater? The company has a greater opportunity to make a profit from its customer, over and over.

11 The other eight strategies are much more complicated; they include formulas that calculate, among other things, a company's gross margins, net margins, and cash-flow ratio. The ten women in the investment club learned what those financial terms mean, as well as how to use the formulas—an impressive accomplishment. But did they make money?

12 In the first year of the investment club, the women bought stocks in ten U.S. companies. How did their stocks do compared with other stocks? From September to December of that year, the value of stocks in the 500 largest U.S. companies (the companies known as the "S&P 500") went up 8.16 percent. But the value of the stocks the women bought went up 17 percent.

13 The women claim that their main goal in forming the investment club was not to become millionaires, but to learn. Apparently they learned a lot. It will be interesting to see, years from now, just how big their nest eggs are.

BUILDING VOCABULARY

UNDERSTANDING SPECIALIZED TERMS

The words below are from the stories "A Smart Investor" and "How to Build a Nest Egg." Put each word in the right category. Write your answers on the lines.

CEO	investment strategy	money manager	stock holder
consumer	leader in its field	stockbroker	stock portfolio
investor	leading company	stock certificates	top dog
investments			

1. people

   investor

2. ways of describing a successful company

   leading company

3. what a stockholder has

   investment strategy

DEVELOPING READING SKILLS

UNDERSTANDING THE MAIN IDEAS

A reporter who interviewed Karin Housely asked the questions below. How do you think Karin Housely might have answered the questions? Write your answers on a separate piece of paper. The first one is done for you.

1. Your husband is a professional hockey player and earns a good salary, yet you were worried about your family's financial future. Why?

   My husband was making a lot of money, but we weren't saving any of it. We spent every penny he made. So I was worried about the future. What if my husband got sick or injured and couldn't work? How would we pay for our children's educations? Would we have enough money when we retired? These were some of the things I was worried about.

2. Tell me a little about your investment club. Who's in it? How does it work?
3. How are your stocks doing so far?

PARAPHRASING

Paraphrasing is expressing in your own words what someone has written or said, usually in a way that is shorter or clearer. Paraphrasing what you have read is a good way to check your comprehension. Also, re-reading your paraphrase is a good way to review before a test. You will find that it is not difficult to paraphrase material that you have understood well.

Re-read paragraphs 4–10 of "How to Build a Nest Egg." Paraphrase the women's four investment strategies. Write your answers on a separate piece of paper. The first one is done for you.

1. Buy What You Know. *(paragraphs 4–5)*

   If you are thinking about stocks, think first about companies that you like. Look around your home and notice which brands you buy—which toothpaste or soft drinks, for example. That doesn't mean that you go out and buy stocks in those companies. But it's a good way to get a list of possible companies to invest in.

2. K.I.S.S. (Keep It Super Simple.) *(paragraph 6)*
3. Leader in Its Field. *(paragraph 7)*
4. Repeat Profitability. *(paragraphs 8–10)*

READING A BAR GRAPH

A Read the following paragraph.

Money managers admit that investing in the stock market has its risks; still, many say it is the best long-term investment in the United States—better than investing in bonds,[1] better than investing in gold, and certainly better than not investing money at all. They give the example of four people who each had $1,000 to invest in 1964. One person put the money under the mattress for safekeeping; one person bought gold; one person bought bonds; and one person bought stocks. This is how much money each person had in 1997, 33 years later:

- The person who put the money under a mattress still had $1,000 (although it would buy less than it did in 1964 because of inflation).
- The person who bought gold had $8,086.
- The person who bought bonds had $11,990.
- The person who bought stocks had $30,934.

1 *Bonds* are pieces of paper you buy from a government (U.S. savings bonds, for example) or from a company. After a certain period of time, the government or company pays you back with interest. The longer the period of time, the higher the interest rate is.

B **The information from the paragraph in Exercise A is represented in the bar graph below. Some information is missing from the graph. Read the paragraph again. Write the missing information in the graph.**

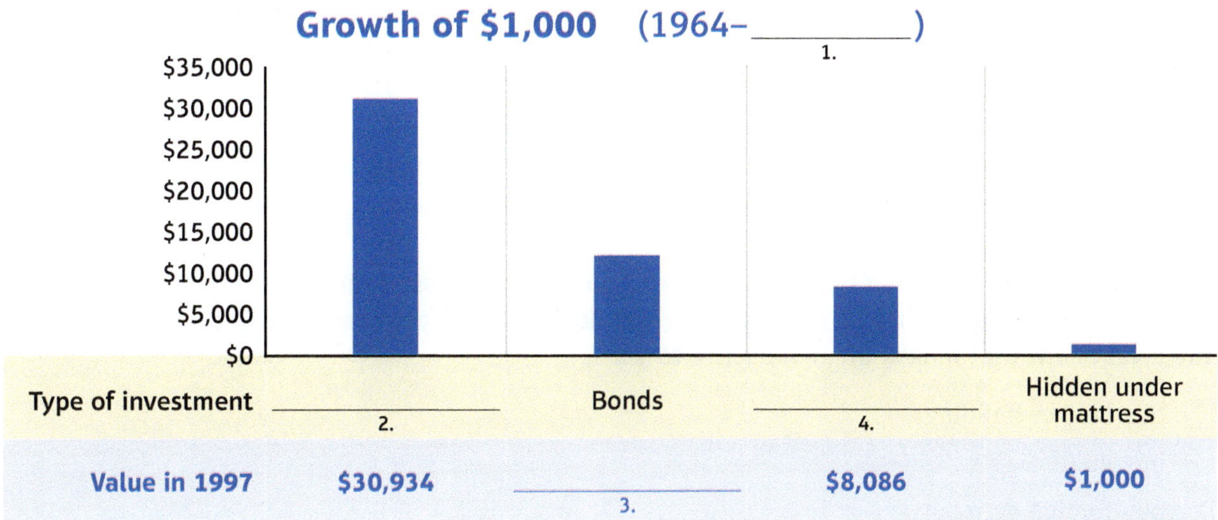

C **Discuss your answers with your classmates.**

1. The graph shows the growth of $1,000 from 1964 to 1997. Do you think the graph might look different if it showed the growth of $1,000 invested for a shorter period of time—for example, 1964 to 1969? How might it be different?
2. Is there another type of investment that you would like to see compared with the stock market in the graph? What is it?
3. Money managers admit that the stock market is not without its risks. If you had $1,000 to invest, would you take the risk of investing it in the stock market? Why or why not?

DISCUSSION

One of the strategies the women in the investment club used was "buy what you know." Do you have any favorite brands? Are there brands you always buy, even though another brand is cheaper?

A **On a separate piece of paper, make a list of your five favorite brands. Show your list to a partner. Explain to your partner why you like these brands.**

B **Write the name of the first company that comes to your mind when you hear the words below.**

car	________	tea	________
shoes	________	coffee	________
chocolate	________	technology	________
soft drink	________	jeans	________
detergent	________	fast food	________
toothpaste	________	airline	________
video game	________		

C Compare your answers with your classmates'. Did you and your classmates name any of the same companies? Do you think these companies are "top dogs"?

D From your list on page 113, choose one company whose stock you would like to buy. (The company might be part of a bigger company.) Find out how much stock in that company costs per share. At a later date, check the price of "your" stock.

E Almost half of all families in the United States have money invested in the stock market. How do people in your country invest money? Tell the class.

F Imagine this: You have saved some money. You want to invest your money so that years from now you will have a nest egg. How would you invest your savings? Check (✓) the investment that makes the most sense to you.

- ☐ buy land or buildings
- ☐ buy gold
- ☐ buy foreign currency
- ☐ put the money in a savings account in a bank
- ☐ buy government bonds
- ☐ invest in the stock market
- ☐ invest in mutual funds (you buy stock in a group of companies that a mutual fund company chooses for you)
- ☐ ______________________________ (other)

G Tell the class why you checked the investment you did.

WRITING

Choose one of the following topics to write about.

1. Do you know anyone who, like Anne Scheiber, invested money and became rich? Or do you know anyone who invested money and lost it? Write the story.
2. Anne Scheiber concluded that the surest way to get rich was to invest in stocks. What do you think is the surest way to get rich?
3. Research one of the following: the U.S. stock market crash of 1929, the Great Depression that followed it, or the Great Recession of 2008. Write a report on what you learned.
4. The title of Anne Scheiber's story is "A Smart Investor." Do you think Anne Scheiber was smart? Explain your answer.

UNIT 8

Helping One Another

In this unit, you will think about why people help one another. But first, you will think about times when people have helped you.

A **Use the questions below to interview a partner. Check (✓) your partner's answers. Then change roles.**

Has anyone ever	Yes	No
1. loaned you money?	☐	☐
2. helped you change a flat tire?	☐	☐
3. helped you with your homework?	☐	☐
4. given you a ride home?	☐	☐
5. loaned you a tool?	☐	☐
6. loaned you a book?	☐	☐
7. helped you when you were sick?	☐	☐
8. given you directions when you were lost?	☐	☐
9. helped you move into a new home?	☐	☐
10. helped you find a job?	☐	☐
11. helped you make a difficult decision?	☐	☐
12. listened while you talked about your problems?	☐	☐

B **Tell your partner about a time you were helped.**

In this unit, you will first read the true story of a man whose life was saved by a stranger in World War II. Then you will learn how most social psychologists in the West would answer the question, "Why do people help others?"

A TRUE STORY IN THE NEWS

PRE-READING

The man in the photo is looking at a memorial. It is dedicated to Filipino and U.S. soldiers who died in the Philippines during World War II. The next story is about a soldier who fought there. His name is not on the memorial; he survived the war.

A **Look at the photo and read the title of the story on the next page. With your classmates, make a list of questions you think the story will answer.**

Example:

1. What was the soldier's name?
2. What country was he from?

B **When you have finished reading the story, look back at the questions you and your classmates wrote. Which questions did the story answer?**

Chosen

1 In 1940, a year before the United States entered World War II, Irvin Scott volunteered for service in the U.S. Marines. He was 19 years old, six feet tall, and weighed 170 pounds. In 1945, when the war ended, he weighed 98 pounds, after spending almost the entire war as a prisoner of the Japanese. His survival was due partly to his own strength, both physical and mental, and partly to the kindness of two men—a Japanese guard and an American comrade.

2 After the United States entered the war in December 1941, Scott was sent to the Bataan Peninsula in the Philippines. He was with a special radar unit that tried to detect incoming Japanese planes. Four months later, the Philippine islands were taken by the Japanese military, and Scott, along with thousands of other American servicemen, surrendered. Eventually, Scott was sent to Tayabas, a province on the island of Luzon in the Philippines. He and the other 300 American prisoners of war at Tayabas were ordered to finish building a road that the U.S. military had begun. Tayabas is located in the jungle, where the combination of heat, rain, and mosquitoes made the conditions ideal for the spread of malaria. Over 100 of the 300 Americans died in the first three months at Tayabas. The prisoners who came down with malaria would lie outside on rocks in the pouring rain, seeking relief from their fevers.

3 Scott, too, came down with malaria, but remained strong enough to work. One day, he sat down to rest at the side of the road he was helping to build. In an attempt to keep his spirits up, he began to hum the aria "Un Bel Di" from the opera *Madame Butterfly*, his mother's favorite. As he sat at the roadside and hummed, Scott heard footsteps behind him and then a voice—the voice of a Japanese guard who said, "I know that song." The guard explained in English that when he was a teenager in Japan, he had worked for an American couple who had played a recording of "Un Bel Di." *Madame Butterfly* had been their favorite opera, too. Scott never turned around as the guard spoke; guards and prisoners were not allowed to communicate, and Scott knew that if he and the guard were seen talking, both men's lives would be in danger. The guard finished speaking, and Scott heard the soft thud of something being dropped. When Scott turned around, the guard was gone. On the ground, there was a banana leaf wrapped around rice and a banana.

4 The Japanese guard was on duty every other day. Every time he was on duty, he managed to pass Scott, and, as he did, he dropped some food wrapped in a banana leaf. Apparently the guard was sharing his lunch with his American prisoner. The guard never spoke to Scott, and Scott never spoke to him. Scott never even learned the guard's name.

5 Several weeks later, Scott, whose malaria had worsened, passed out on the road he was working on. A fellow prisoner of war, Bill White, whom Scott did not know, carried him back to the camp—an act of heroism, as Bill White, like Scott, was sick and weak. Every few hours, White would carry Scott down to a creek to bathe him in cool water to try to bring his fever down. He fed him a mixture of rice and water the prisoners made, as well as the food the Japanese guard continued to drop at Scott's side. White also gave Scott quinine tablets for the malaria.

6 At first, Scott was too delirious with fever to realize what he was being fed, but when he was stronger, he asked White where he had gotten the quinine tablets. White told Scott to wait until the afternoon, and to keep an eye on the guard.

7 Irvin Scott, who was over 80 years old when he told the following story, remembered clearly what he saw that afternoon: "This Japanese guard came walking across the rocks. All the prisoners were lying out on the rocks, dying or barely able to move because of the malaria. As the guard passed by, he dropped something wrapped in a banana leaf. He kept walking and said nothing. Bill unwrapped the leaf, and in it was some rice and a little piece of paper. Inside the paper were two tablets of quinine."

continued ▶

8 With the help of Bill White and the food and quinine from the Japanese guard, Scott eventually regained some strength. He and Bill White were at Tayabas for the entire summer of 1942; then they were sent to a former American Army base near Manila that had been captured by the Japanese. They were there for about two years, and during that time Scott and White became close friends.

9 In 1944, Irvin Scott and Bill White were sent to Japan aboard separate ships. White's ship was sunk by torpedoes, but Scott's ship continued on to Japan. He worked in a coal mine there until the war ended in 1945 and then returned to the United States aboard a hospital ship.

10 Long after the war, Scott continued to think about Tayabas. He thought about Bill White, who fed him the quinine tablets that the guard dropped. White had malaria, too, and no one would have known if he had swallowed the medicine instead of giving it to Scott. Scott also thought about the Japanese guard. The two quinine tablets were half the guard's ration of four tablets, so the guard was risking dying of malaria himself. That, however, was the smaller risk: If the guard's superiors had seen him dropping the food and medicine, he would have been shot.

11 Scott could only speculate why, of all the prisoners at Tayabas, the guard chose to save him. "Who knows why he did it," Scott said. "I don't know to this day. He had to know something was wrong with what was happening. He had compassion, and I was the one he decided to help. I can only think it was because he heard me humming the melody 'Un Bel Di'."

12 Scott had a custom license plate on his car that said *P.O.W.*—prisoner of war. The license plate was a reminder of all the hardships he had endured. Yet Scott did not hate the Japanese. On the contrary, he said the Japanese were "good human beings." What is the explanation for Scott's lack of hatred? Did he recognize that in war there is suffering on both sides—and that Japanese had suffered at the hands of the Americans, just as he had suffered at the hands of the Japanese? Perhaps he did. But there is also a simpler explanation: Scott found it impossible to hate the Japanese because of the kindness and courage of one Japanese guard. Scott's car—the one with the *P.O.W.* license plate—was a Honda Accord.

Prisoner of War medal

GETTING THE BIG PICTURE

Why is the story titled "Chosen"? Circle the letter of your answer.

a. In 1940, Scott volunteered for service in the U.S Marines. Because he was strong both physically and mentally, he was chosen for a special radar unit.

b. Scott was a prisoner of war for four years. Because of all he endured, he has chosen not to talk about his experiences.

c. Of all the prisoners at the camp, the Japanese guard chose to save Scott. Because of the guard's help, Scott was able to survive the war.

BUILDING VOCABULARY

RECALLING NEW WORDS

The words below are from the story. Complete each sentence with the correct word or words.

attempt	endured	managed to	speculated
delirious	keep an eye on	pass out	surrendered
due to	lack	relief	volunteered

1. In 1940, the United States was not yet at war, so American men did not have to be soldiers. Irvin Scott, however, wanted to be a soldier, so he ___volunteered___ for service in the U.S. Marines.

2. Scott did not die because he was strong physically and mentally. His survival was also ____________ the help of two men—a Japanese guard and an American comrade.

3. When the Japanese took the Philippines, U.S. soldiers put down their guns and stopped fighting. They ____________ in 1942.

4. There were no doctors or medicine to help the sick prisoners; the only way they could find ____________ from their fevers was to lie on the rocks when it rained.

5. Scott tried to stay mentally strong. In an ____________ to keep his spirits up, he hummed his mother's favorite song.

6. It was dangerous and difficult for the Japanese guard to give food to Scott, but he succeeded in doing it. He ____________ drop food every other day.

7. Scott fainted while working. Bill White saw him ____________ and carried him back to camp.

8. When he was sick with malaria, Scott didn't know where he was or what was happening around him. Sometimes he thought he was home in his own bed; sometimes he saw his mother standing beside him. He was ____________ with fever.

9. Scott watched the Japanese guard as he walked across the rocks because Bill White told him to ____________________ the guard.

10. Scott didn't know why the guard chose to help him; he could only guess at the reason. He ____________________ the guard helped him because he was humming "Un Bel Di."

11. Scott suffered very much when he was a prisoner of war. His license plate, *P.O.W.*, was a reminder of all he ____________________.

12. Scott had no hatred for the Japanese. What is the explanation for his ____________________ of hatred?

USING NEW WORDS

A **Complete the sentences below with examples from your own life.**

1. To get relief when I am under a lot of stress, I ____________________.
2. I lack ____________________.
3. I would never attempt to ____________________.
4. Although it was difficult, I managed to ____________________.
5. I would volunteer immediately if someone asked for help with ____________________.
6. People sometimes pass out when ____________________.

B **In a small group, take turns reading your sentences aloud. Ask your classmates questions about their sentences.**

DEVELOPING READING SKILLS

UNDERSTANDING THE MAIN IDEAS

There is one correct way to complete each sentence. Circle the letter of the correct answer.

1. This story is about an American prisoner of war
   a. who saved the lives of over 100 soldiers at a camp in the Philippines.
   (b.) whose life was saved by a Japanese guard and an American comrade.
   c. who died in the Philippines during the final month of World War II.
2. Irvin Scott was a prisoner of war
   a. for the entire summer of 1942.
   b. from 1942 to 1945.
   c. for several weeks in 1941.
3. The Japanese guard helped Scott by
   a. allowing him to escape.
   b. sending him to a hospital.
   c. dropping food and medicine.

4. Bill White helped Scott when he was sick by
   a. writing letters to his family.
   b. doing Scott's work for him.
   c. bathing him in cool water and giving him food and medicine.
5. Scott believed that the Japanese guard chose to save him because
   a. he liked Americans.
   b. he reminded him of an American man he had worked for.
   c. he heard him humming "Un Bel Di," a song that he knew.
6. Scott did not hate the Japanese because
   a. of the kindness and courage of the Japanese guard.
   b. many Japanese people had helped him during the war.
   c. he had lived with a Japanese couple when he was a teenager.

IDENTIFYING TIME EXPRESSIONS

To show the passing of time, writers use time expressions. These time expressions tell you when events occurred, how often they occurred, or for how long they occurred. The writer of "Chosen" uses many time expressions, such as "in 1944" and "four months later," to show the passing of time.

Complete each sentence by matching the time expression with an event. Write the letter of your answer on the line.

Time Expression

1. In 1940, __f__
2. In the first three months at Tayabas, _____
3. Every other day, _____
4. Eventually, _____
5. Until the war ended in 1945, _____
6. Long after the war, _____

Event

a. Scott worked in a coal mine in Japan.
b. Scott continued to think about Bill White and the Japanese guard.
c. Scott recovered from malaria and regained some strength.
d. the Japanese guard dropped food and medicine for Scott.
e. over 100 Americans died.
f. Irvin Scott volunteered for service in the U.S. Marines.

MAKING INFERENCES

Sometimes writers do not state information directly. Then we have to use information they do give to make an *inference*—to make a logical guess. For example, the story does not tell us if Bill White survived the war. It does tell us, however, that his ship was sunk by torpedoes. So, we can infer that he did not survive the war, even though the writer does not state this directly.

The answers to the questions below are not in the story. Use the information you have to make a good guess.

1. In 1940, Irvin Scott weighed 170 pounds; in 1945, he weighed 98 pounds. What does that tell you about the amount of food he was given when he was a prisoner of war?

   He probably did not get much food.

2. The Japanese guard shared his lunch—some rice and a banana. What does that tell you about the food the Japanese soldiers in the Philippines had?

3. If the guard's superiors had seen him dropping food, he would have been shot. What does that tell you about the character of the guard?

4. Irvin Scott returned to the United States aboard a hospital ship. What does that tell you about his physical condition at that time?

5. Why do you think Scott's humming "Un Bel Di" made the guard decide to save him?

NEWS AND VIEWS

Long after the war, Irvin Scott continued to think about the Japanese guard who gave him food and medicine. "Who knows why he did it?" Scott asked. "I don't know to this day."

A **Why do people help one another? Before you read the article below, think about this statement:**

People help other people because they want something in return.

B **Put an *X* on the line below near the word *agree* if you think the statement above is true, near the word *disagree* if you think it is not true, and somewhere between the two words if your opinion is somewhere in between.**

agree •• disagree

C **Now read the article below.**

Helping Behavior

Why Do We Help Others?

1 Why do people help one another? Why do we stop to help a stranger change a flat tire? Why do we stay up all night comforting a friend? Why do we drop coins into a beggar's cup? Why do we give our money, time, possessions, and even our lives to others?

2 Social psychologists—scholars who study how people influence one another's thoughts, feelings, and behavior—think about questions like these. They have concluded that we give to other people because we get something in return. All helping acts, they say, ultimately help the helper. Sometimes the rewards for helping are external, and sometimes they are internal, but there are always rewards.

3 External rewards come from other people. We loan a classmate a pen, and she loans us a pen when we need one. We give the boss a ride in the hope of getting a promotion. We erase the board for the teacher in the hope of getting a good grade. A wealthy couple gives money for cancer research, and a new clinic is named in their honor.

4 Internal rewards are those we give ourselves. When we help others, we congratulate ourselves for being kind; we avoid feeling guilty or ashamed; and we relieve the distress we feel at seeing someone else in distress. Or perhaps helping others makes us feel superior to those we help, or it makes us feel connected to other people.

5 The idea that everyone's ultimate goal is to benefit himself or herself—even while helping others—is called egoism. It is the view held by the majority of social psychologists in the Western world. There is, however, a small minority of social psychologists who believe that sometimes people help others without wanting anything in return. This type of helping behavior is called altruism.

6 While social psychologists do not agree on what motivates people to help—egoism or altruism—they do agree that people are more likely to help under some circumstances and less likely to help under others.

When Do We Help Others?

7 **The bystander effect.** In 1964, people in the United States were shocked to hear this story: At 3 a.m., a young woman named Kitty

continued ▶

Genovese was walking home from work in New York City when a man caught and stabbed her. She screamed for help, and lights came on in several nearby apartments. Thirty-eight people saw the crime from their apartment windows, but only one person called the police, and the call came too late. Kitty Genovese died.

8 Although the story was reported in many reputable newspapers, it turned out later that it wasn't completely true. There was a murder, but thirty-eight people had not seen it and done nothing. Many people said they had heard something, but they weren't sure what they were hearing—maybe a couple arguing, or a drunk. And two people, not one, called the police. One 70-year-old woman came out of her apartment to see if she could help. She held Kitty until the police arrived.

9 When the story was first reported, people didn't know it wasn't completely true, and it shocked them. Why had no one helped Kitty Genovese? Social psychologists heard the same story everyone else did. They, too, wondered why no one had helped. They speculated that people tend not to help when a lot of other people are around. To test that theory, they did several scientific experiments.

10 One of the best-known experiments is called the "Lady in Distress." In this experiment, a female experimenter asked college students to fill out a questionnaire. The experimenter left the room, saying she would return when the students had finished the questionnaire. Then the experimenter pretended that she had an accident in the next room. The students heard the sound of a chair being moved, followed by a loud scream and a crash. Next, they heard the woman crying and moaning, "Oh, my foot... I...can't move it. Oh...my ankle...I can't get this thing off me." The cries continued for about a minute and then stopped.

11 Would the students come to the woman's aid? When students were alone in the room, 70 percent of them went into the next room to see if the woman needed help. But when students were in the room with another student, only 20 percent offered help (Latané & Rodin, 1969).

12 The "Lady in Distress" experiment prompted social psychologists to come to this conclusion: As the number of bystanders (people who witness a crime or an accident) increases, offers of help decrease. This relationship between the number of bystanders and offers of help is called the "bystander effect."

13 **Other factors that influence helping behavior.** Further experiments demonstrated that dozens of factors influence whether or not people help. For example, people are more likely to help when someone else helps first. Even the weather has an influence. (People are more likely to help on sunny days.) With so many factors affecting helping behavior, how can social psychologists predict with certainty when people will help? They cannot. They can only make general predictions about helping behavior. For example, social psychologists say the bystander effect holds true most of the time. So, if you are alone in a city and need help, ask a person standing alone rather than a person in a group.

Summary

14 For decades, social psychologists have been studying helping behavior. They have been trying to answer primarily two questions:

15 1. Why do we help others? Some social psychologists believe we help for selfish, egoistic reasons: Helping benefits us. Sometimes the reward is external, and sometimes it is internal, but there is always a reward for helping. Other social psychologists believe that sometimes we help for altruistic reasons, expecting no reward.

16 2. When do we help others? Generally speaking, we are more likely to help others when we are alone than when we are with other bystanders. However, there are many other factors that affect helping behavior.

References

Latané, B., & Rodin, J. (1969) A lady in distress: Inhibiting effects of friends and strangers on bystander intervention. *Journal of Experimental Social Psychology* 5, 189–202.

BUILDING VOCABULARY

UNDERSTANDING ACADEMIC VOCABULARY

The words below are on the Academic Word List. Find the words in "Helping Behavior." (The number in parentheses is the number of the paragraph.) If you are not sure what a word means, look it up in your dictionary. Then use the words in the sentences that follow.

concluded (2)	benefit (5)	factors (13)	decade (14)
external (2)	circumstances (6)	predicted (13)	affected (16)
goal (5)	theory (9)		

1. Rub the medicine on your face, but don't let any get into your mouth. The medicine is for ___external___ use only.
2. Unfortunately, they met when she was leaving and he was arriving; if __________ had been different, they might have become good friends.
3. His __________ is to be the owner of a small business by the time he is 30.
4. When she was a child, her grandfather __________ that she would be an actress someday, and he was right.
5. There are many __________ that influence the university's decision to admit a student; test scores and high school grades are only two of them.
6. When he moved from Mexico to Canada, he noticed that the long, dark winters __________ his mood; he sometimes became sad during the winter months.
7. After carefully comparing the two students' exams, the teacher __________ that one student must have copied the other student's answers.
8. Scientists in Great Britain thought that perhaps a million children jumping up and down at the same moment could cause a small earthquake. To test the __________, thousands of schoolchildren jumped up and down at 11 a.m. on September 7, 2001. (The jumping children did cause very small earthquakes.)
9. She decided to work in a hospital for a year before going to medical school because she thought she would __________ from the real-life experience.
10. In the United States, the __________ from 1920 to 1930 is called "The Roaring Twenties."

RECOGNIZING DEFINITIONS

In a textbook, there are many *terms*—words and expressions that are common in a particular field. These terms are often defined within the reading. As you read, it is important to recognize definitions. Here are three ways to recognize a definition in English:

- a dash before and after the definition (or sometimes only before the definition)
- a form of the verb *to be*
- the expression *is called*

A **Find these five terms—*social psychologists, egoism, altruism, internal rewards, external rewards,* and *the bystander effect*—on pages 123–124 and circle them. Notice how the writer of the article helps you recognize the definitions of these words.**

B **Look at the chart below. Some terms and definitions are missing. Fill in the missing information.**

Terms	Definitions
1. social psychologists	scholars who study how people influence one another's thoughts, feelings, and behavior
2. ______	rewards that come from other people
internal rewards	3. ______
4. ______	the idea that everyone's ultimate goal in helping others is to benefit himself or herself
altruism	5. ______
6. ______	the relationship between the number of bystanders and offers of help

DEVELOPING READING SKILLS

MAKING AN OUTLINE

Outlines can help you remember the main ideas and supporting details of a chapter in a textbook. Before a test, you can study your outline rather than study the textbook. Below is an informal outline a student might make after reading "Helping Behavior." Notice how the subheadings of the article became part of the outline.

Some information is missing from the outline below. Complete the outline with information from the article "Helping Behavior."

Helping Behavior

I. Why do we help others?

A. Majority of social psychologists in the West: We help other people because we get something in ___return___ (1.). This is called ________ (2.).

Two types of rewards for helping:

1. External rewards come from other ________ (3.). Examples:

—Giving the boss a ride home to get a ________ (4.).

—Erasing the board for the teacher to get a good ________ (5.).

2. ________ (6.) rewards—those we give ourselves. Examples:

—We ________ (7.) ourselves for being kind.

—We avoid feeling ________ (8.) or ashamed.

B. ________ (9.) of social psychologists: Sometimes people ________ (10.) others without wanting anything in return. This type of helping behavior is called ________ (11.).

II. When do we help others?

A. The bystander ________ (12.): As the number of bystanders increases, offers of help ________ (13.). Example: The "Lady in ________ (14.)" experiment

B. Other factors that influence helping behavior:

—Someone else helping first

—Sunny ________ (15.)

READING A GRAPH

Sociologist Paul Amato studied helping behavior by doing an experiment in the United States. The results are recorded in the graph below. With your classmates, study the graph and answer the questions.

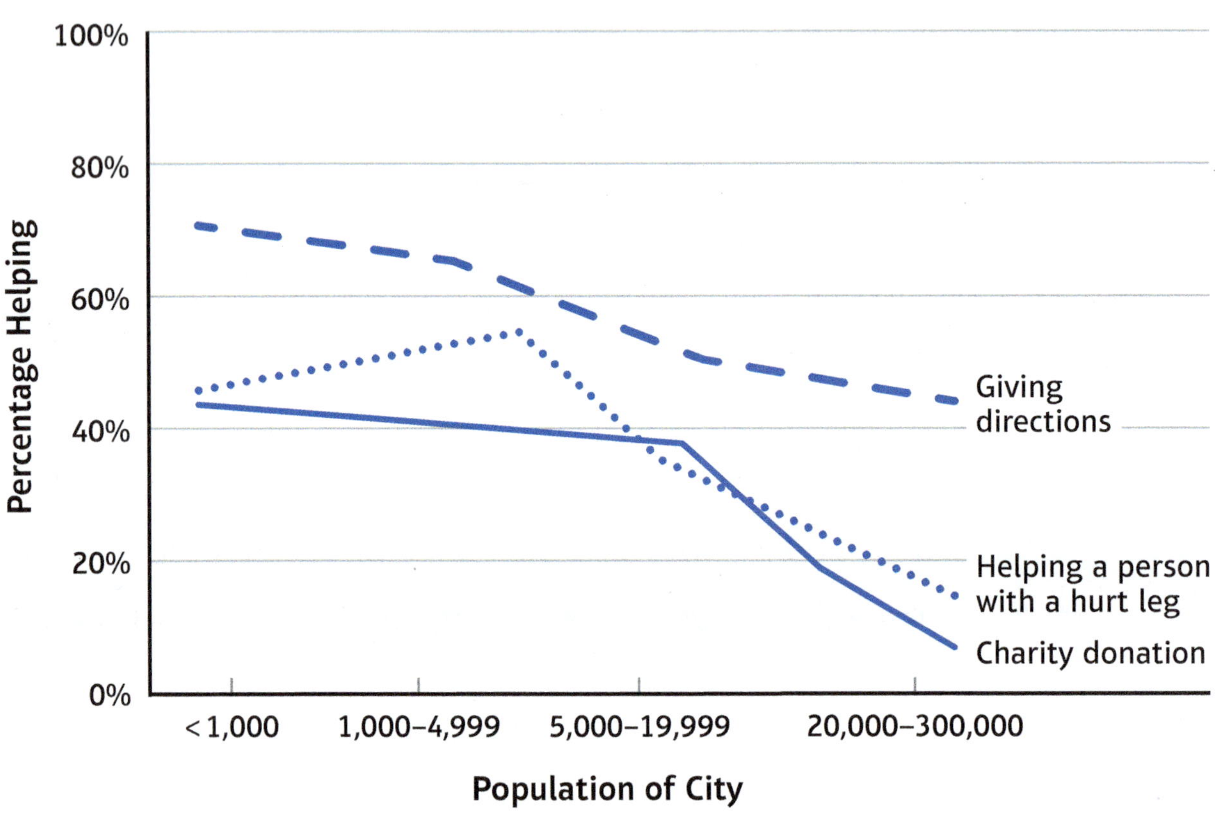

1. What do you think the sociologist wanted to learn from the experiment?
2. What were the results of the experiment?
3. Did the results of the experiment surprise you?
4. If you did the same experiment in your country, do you think the results would be the same?

DISCUSSION

A **Think about these questions. Discuss your answers with your classmates.**

1. The Japanese guard risked his life for Scott. Can you think of other examples of people who risked their lives for strangers, perhaps during a war or during a time of persecution? Tell the class what you know about these people.
2. What possible rewards did the Japanese guard get for helping?
3. Social psychologist C. Daniel Batson believes that altruism exists—that people sometimes help others without wanting anything in return. He believes his experiments prove that people will help for altruistic reasons when they think the person needing help is like them in some way. How do you think Dr. Batson would explain the behavior of the Japanese guard?

B **In a group of three, choose one of the following three stories about people who helped others. Read it silently, and summarize it for the other two people in your group.**

Sandra Andersen

Sandra Andersen worked at a coffee shop in Seattle. One of her favorite customers was Annamarie Ausnes. Annamarie stopped by every morning on her way to work for a cup of coffee to go. She was always cheerful and fun to talk to.

One morning, Annamarie wasn't her usual self, and Sandra asked her if anything was wrong. Actually, Annamarie said, there was something wrong. She needed a kidney transplant, and no one in her family was a match as a donor.

"I'll get tested," Sandra said, and she did. It turned out that Sandra's blood type matched Annamarie's perfectly. A short time later, doctors removed one of Sandra's kidneys and transplanted it into Annamarie. Both women are doing fine.

Robert Gomez and Jesse Orach

Robert Gomez was running in a 10-kilometer race. At the beginning of the race, he thought he had a good chance of winning. But he couldn't keep up with the runner ahead of him, Jesse Orach. He realized that Jesse would probably come in first, and he would come in second.

When Robert came around a turn at the end of the race, he saw Jesse lying on the grass just 90 meters (100 yards) from the finish line. He had collapsed from dehydration. Robert had only seconds to decide what to do—run around Jesse and win the race, or stop to help him.

Robert helped Jesse to his feet and held him up as both runners ran to the finish line. Then Robert pushed Jesse across the finish line ahead of him. Jesse won the race and got the $1,000 prize. Robert came in second and received $500.

Keshia Thomas

Fifteen members of the Ku Klux Klan, a small, extremist group that promotes hatred toward certain races and religious groups, were marching through the streets of Ann Arbor, Michigan. One thousand people who opposed the group came to shout at them. Suddenly, some people in the group of 1,000 began beating one of the Ku Klux Klan members.

Keshia Thomas, an 18-year-old African American woman, fell on top of the man who was being beaten and shielded him with her body. The man survived and had only minor injuries.

C Think about these questions. Discuss your answers with your classmates.

1. What possible external or internal rewards could Sandra Andersen, Robert Gomez, and Keshia Thomas have gotten from helping?
2. Do the actions of Robert Gomez and Keshia Thomas support the "bystander effect"? Explain your answer.
3. Do any of these stories remind you of a similar story? Tell your story to the class.

WRITING

Irvin Scott, the prisoner of war, was helped by strangers. Most of the time, though, help comes not from strangers, but from people we know well—from parents, sisters, brothers, friends, neighbors, and teachers.

A Read the lyrics to the song "Because You Loved Me" on the Internet. If possible, listen to Celine Dion's recording of the song as you read. Then write a short essay about a person who helped you. For example, you could explain how someone "made your dream come true" or "gave you strength when you were weak."

B Find out about a volunteer organization in your community, and do one of the following writing assignments.

1. In a short report, summarize what the organization does.
2. Interview someone who volunteers at the organization. Find out what they do and why they do it. Write a report on what you learned.

KEY TO GUESSED ANSWERS

UNIT 1

DISCUSSION page 15

B

	Steps	Stars
1.	Don't overdo alcohol.	★★★★★
2.	Don't use illegal drugs, like heroin or cocaine.	
3.	Eat more fruits and vegetables—five to seven per day.	★★★★★
4.	Cut the amount of fat in your diet.	★★★★★
5.	Fasten seat belts.	★★★★
6.	Develop skills for coping with stress.	★★★★★
7.	Get enough sleep.	★★★
8.	Take care of your teeth and gums.	★★★
9.	Have a sense of humor.	★★★★
10.	Build good relationships with friends.	★★★★
11.	Own a pet.	★★
12.	Make your workplace fun.	★★★

UNIT 3

DISCUSSION pages 48–49

B

1. **True** One company offers eight-week programming courses in places like Playa del Carmen, Mexico; Barcelona, Spain; and Lake Tahoe, California.
2. **True** For example, MIT, a university in the United States, offers a non-credit class in table manners, dressing for success, and behavior in social situations. Potsdam University in Germany offers a class that helps future information technology engineers impress people at parties and "flirt."
3. **False** In a poll of 17,800 geeks, only 12% said they type more slowly than most people they know.
4. **True** The organization was founded in London and is now in 23 countries.
5. **True** In 2006, Spanish blogger Germán Martínez wrote about his idea to dedicate a day celebrating geeks. He suggested May 25, the day the first *Star Wars* film was released in 1977. His idea spread across the Internet, and today many countries celebrate Geek Pride Day on May 25.
6. **True** Oversized eyeglasses are one of the accessories recommended for men and women wanting to dress like geeks.

F

1. **Eye candy** — images on a computer screen that are attractive to look at
2. **Scareware** — a computer program that tricks users into downloading software that could be dangerous—that contains a virus, for example
3. **Treeware** — material that is printed on paper—for example, an owner's manual or a newspaper
4. **TLDR** — too long; didn't read
5. **UX** — user experience
6. **Content farm** — a Web site that has a lot of information, most of it of poor quality and taken from other Web sites

UNIT 4

DISCUSSION page 67

D

1. Tom got letters and e-mail from people all over the world. (Some women wrote him that they looked exactly like the woman in the picture. The problem was that they were already married.) He spent thousands of dollars and drove thousands of miles to meet women who looked like his "dream girl." He met a lot of women but, after talking with them, decided they were not his soul mate. Perhaps he is still looking for her.

UNIT 5

DISCUSSION page 84

B

2. Craig Karges says there is no magic in the way the pendulum works; you are making the pendulum swing. He explains with this example: "Imagine you're driving down the highway and you're late for an appointment. You think to yourself, 'I'm going to be really late, I've got to get there.' All of a sudden you look at your speedometer and see you're going 80 miles an hour. Your subconscious mind is saying, 'We have to get there! Step on it!' You don't consciously feel yourself putting extra pressure on the gas pedal, but you are. Your subconscious mind is sending a message down to your foot, and your foot presses down on the gas pedal." The pendulum works the same way: Your subconscious mind, where your intuition is buried, sends a signal to your body to control the swinging of the pendulum.

UNIT 6

DISCUSSION page 99

B

1. The bratwurst feud went to Germany's highest court. The court ruled that the man could grill sausages only five times each summer.
2. Neighbors and the church fought over the soup kitchen for five years. Finally, the case went to court. The judge said the kitchen could open. The day the kitchen opened, 150 people came for a free breakfast, ate quietly, and left. There were no problems.